THE NO-NONSENSE GUIDE
TO THE SIXTH SENSE

Shelley von Strunckel

CORGI BOOKS

THE NO-NONSENSE GUIDE TO THE SIXTH SENSE
A CORGI BOOK 0 552 13484 8

First publication in Great Britain

PRINTING HISTORY
Corgi edition published 1990

Copyright © Shelley von Strunckel 1990

This book is set in 10/11pt Plantin
by Busby Typesetting, Exeter

Corgi Books are published by Transworld Publishers Ltd.,
61–63 Uxbridge Road, Ealing, London W5 5SA, in Australia by
Transworld Publishers (Australia) Pty. Ltd., 15–23 Helles
Avenue, Moorebank, NSW 2170, and in New Zealand by Transworld
Publishers (N.Z.) Ltd., Cnr. Moselle and Waipareira Avenues,
Henderson, Auckland.

Printed and bound in Great Britain by
BPCC Hazell Books Ltd
Member of BPCC Ltd
Aylesbury, Bucks, England

CONTENTS

Page

Part I

1 Introduction   11
Metaphysics old and new; How to use the Guide; Who wants to know about the sixth sense?; But I don't want to know!; Will I become one of those strange people?; Occult worries; Final departure instructions

2 The Myth of Metaphysics   18
The choice: destiny or free will; What about destiny?; Free will for you?; Whose responsibility is it?; Making your choice; Do you want to be rescued?

3 Now That You're Here, Get to Know the Ropes   24
Expectations; The readers' responsibility; Clients' responsibilities and rights

4 You're On Your Own – Making a Choice   30
Why a guide is necessary; Finding the best; How to find a reader; What speciality of reader to see?; Where do readers come from?; Are readers special people?; Can you trust your reader?; The fringe element; How to prepare for your visit to a reader; Exploring the book; Packing for your trip

5 You Want to Do It Yourself   40
Deeper study; Becoming a consultant; Techniques to try out; Words of warning; Areas not to be experimented with; Metaphysical chat; Bon voyage!

Part II

6 Astrological Surprise   51
  *What's pop astrology?; Consulting astrology; Where astro-
  logy came from; Astrological identity crisis; New twist to
  old science; How to judge a magazine column; Year by
  year; A whole magazine full of astrology!; Computerised
  perfection?; Is there an astrologer behind astrology?; Taking
  care of business; You make your appointment; Worried
  about words?; Your first time; But I want my fortune told!;
  Astrological tour – different kinds of astrology; Books
  and courses; Studies; Your future with astrology*

7 Cartomancy – the Future from Cards   81
  *Is it really in the cards?; The gypsies' bible?; Fools and
  devils; Symbols in Tarot cards; Interpretation, not reading;
  Playing cards; The lady who was refused a reading; When
  you go; What you can – and can't – find out in a card
  reading; The best the cards have to offer*

8 Clairvoyants and Psychics   95
  *What is clairvoyance?; Are you an intuitive?; Developing
  powers; What psychics see when they look; Animals, oracles
  and scryers; Past perfect; Aura you or aura you not?;
  Repository for all your thoughts; I never thought that!; When
  you go; Cold readings; Finding and selecting a consultant;
  What to ask; The session's not over when it's over; The
  right reader*

9 Spiritualism and Channelling   116
  *(I) Spiritualism: A spirited discussion; Mediums and
  channels – who's who; When you go; What the spirits can
  tell you; The lady whose mother apologised; Spirit reliability;
  Spiritual sensationalism; (II) Channelling: Tuning into the
  right channel; What is on this channel?; How do you tell
  what's good?; What you've been told – when you go; Do
  it yourself?; Otherworldly invitation*

10 Ghosts and Spirits   130

Where ghosts live; Ghostly origins; Ghost stories; Why ghosts clank; A ghost's point of view; Who can talk to ghosts; Nasty ghosts; Ghost fixers; Not quite ghosts – poltergeists; Elementals and devas – spirits of nature; Elementary elementals; Unlike ghosts; Old-time understanding; A modern-day example; Talk to your deva; Mythic elementals

11 Past Lives   141

Reincarnation; Where the idea came from; Getting a grip on past lives; Where do all those souls go?; An old soul?; Suspiciously attractive; Why don't I remember?; Haven't we met before?; How the soul chooses; Settling up over lifetimes; What is karma?; 'Bad' karma and 'good'; Past-life regression; Why do I care about my past lives?; Past-life trap; The unhealed wound; Difficult to prove; The final proof

12 Palmistry and Reading the Body   157

Reading the body; (I) Reading the hand: Palmier days; Is the future in the palm of your hand?; Character and future; The mounting tale; The line-up of lines; Stars in your palm?; When you go; (II) Reading the body: Chinese physiognomy; Phrenology; Moleosophy; Your own body of knowledge

13 Numerology   174

The Greek key to numbers; Cabala's hidden wisdom; Everything has a number; How to get your number; It is all in a name; The meaning of the numbers; Summing it up; If you go – who's really got your number; Can you escape your number?; Do you want to do it yourself?; Making it count

14 Healing   188

What healing is; Where healing happens; What is it that has the power to heal?; Where does the energy go?; Who heals?; Healing history; Faith healing; Classifying healing; Types of healing; Types of healers; Results of healing; Proof; Medicine and healing; If you go; Do-it-yourself healing

15 Magic, Ritual and Spells   204
   *Magic; Worlds of power; The training; Ritual power and
   spells; Rituals; Elements of ritual; Spells; Kinds of spells;
   The power of the mind; Witchcraft in England; Do it
   yourself?; Kinds of magic you can do; Ritual in your life*

16 Objects of Power: Gems, Crystals, Amulets and
   Talismans   221
   *Eye-catching wonders; Old-time charms; Biblical gems;
   Sparkling surprise; Value beyond sparkle; Everyday gems;
   The properties of stones; Birthstones − traditional; Birth-
   stones − contemporary; Crystal clear; Energy absorbers;
   Crystal housekeeping; Put your crystal to work; Programming
   a crystal; Uses for crystals; Where to buy your crystal; How
   to select your crystal; Charms and talismans; Sinister
   shadows; Good luck; Creating luck; A charmed future?*

17 Meditation   238
   *Do you meditate already?; States of mind; I'll meditate on
   that!; Just try concentration; Rosaries and navels; Blood
   pressure and brain waves; Words and sound; Objects of
   contemplation; Mind as mantra; Meditation groups; Pass
   the pretzels; Teachers, gurus and groups; Results; The man
   who knew too much − from meditating; The real reason to
   meditate*

Bibliography   252

PART ONE

1

Introduction

Travelling in a foreign country can be an absolutely
bewildering experience. Exciting as it is, the very foreign-
ness of it can make just figuring out how to make a call
from a public phone an ordeal; and ordering a meal can
have sometimes rather amazing results. In order to avoid
problems like these, even experienced travellers consult a
guidebook before going on a trip to an unfamiliar place,
and keep it with them while travelling. By doing this, they
avoid wasting time and money, and benefit from the
experience (and mistakes) of others who have gone before.
A guidebook offers information that helps avoid making
discoveries about local customs in an embarrassing way,
and, if the customs and language are different, makes it
easier to find the right words at the right time.

METAPHYSICS OLD AND NEW

This is a guide to the kingdom of the sixth sense, the realm
of metaphysics – the land beyond the day-to-day world of
the physical plane. This amazing land extends the full
range of non-physical realms of the present, the past and
the future and to all the beings who live there. For meta-
physicians, those who are familiar with these non-physical
planes, they are as real in their way as the physical one is
in its, and offer a rich world of knowledge and wisdom.

The word Metaphysics derives from Greek *meta ka
physika* and literally means 'after the things of nature'.

11

It was first used by Hellenistic commentators to classify the writings of the Greek philosopher Aristotle which he himself associated with wisdom. When his writings were organised at the Alexandrian Library, those on the nature of the physical world were followed by his speculations on the world beyond the physical, and the general theory of reality. As these writings were catalogued after those on the physical world, they were termed 'metaphysical'.

Over the past several hundred years the term has been most used in two ways, to describe a particular group of philosophers, and also to describe poets whose contemplations on the nature of life were, indeed, metaphysically orientated.

As often happens with terms, it has more recently acquired an additional meaning. Beginning perhaps twenty years ago in the United States, metaphysics began to be used to describe what has been known variously as the paranormal, the occult and more informally 'things that go bump in the night'. Now in common use in the USA, metaphysics has become an umbrella term for all the studies and practices of the worlds of the sixth sense. This has the advantage of including several subjects such as occultism (including ghosts and witchcraft), clairvoyance and the paranormal, which up till recently had to be classified separately.

As a visitor to the land of metaphysics, your stay will be more enjoyable if you understand that this world is governed by considerably different rules from the physical realm. It is even made of different matter from the earthly plane. The laws of space and time there do not function in the same way either. For example, spirits, who are visitors to the physical plane from the astral, another term for the metaphysical, plane, break our rules completely by moving through what appear to be solid walls. Clairvoyants move easily in time between the past and the future. In fact, time itself actually seems to function differently on the metaphysical plane. 'Miracles', such as physical healings, occur at a pace which would be impossible in our 'real' physical plane time.

In the land of metaphysics, in addition to the familiar physical body, each of us has several additional 'metaphysical bodies'. They include the astral body which appears translucent to us on this plane, and is the portion which remains after death, as in the case of ghosts. There is also an etheric body, of yet finer substance than the astral: intuition comes from this body.

In the land of metaphysics, it is also recognised that energy has substance. Thoughts themselves have form and are seen on this plane as we would see a beam of light from a torch at night. Psychics and clairvoyants are able to discern the form of thoughts and, in readings, to tell you about them; in another form the energy of thought is directed by healers to patients.

In the land of metaphysics:

· There is a world beyond the physical plane.
· It is composed of energy, which has substance.
· There is time and space beyond that known in the physical world.
· Each individual has a non-physical as well as a physical body.

HOW TO USE THE *GUIDE*

The metaphysical realm has very different rules and values from those of the earthly plane. The *Guide* explains its complexities. By reading it you can prepare, learn what to expect from each of the areas, what to ask for, where to start your explorations, and some of the language unique to the realm. There are different areas of study, ranging from astrology to card reading, healing, meditation, spells, and past lives. If one of these is already an area of special interest, you may want to start by reading the chapter about it; or stroll at leisure through the chapters to see what is most intriguing.

As fascinating as the metaphysical realm is, many people

are a little hesitant about delving too deeply into it. For most, curiosity is tempered by the sort of anxiety which is produced by unfamiliarity. This caution is not inappropriate: some who have not taken time to prepare for their explorations into the byways of this realm have been disillusioned by its less scrupulous residents. Though these are in the minority, and most who explore any of the lands of metaphysics return rewarded by their experiences, it seems that the charlatans are often more memorable. It takes a little time to learn how to separate fact from fallacy. Profit from others who have gone before, by reading tales of their adventures. Learn what benefits you can expect to derive from visits to various consultants, to be able to evaluate the quality of experts you meet, and have an idea of what fees might be charged and what is reasonable.

And most important, know what to expect in this, the land of the unexpected, so you can enjoy your travels and feel comfortable while making them.

WHO WANTS TO KNOW ABOUT THE SIXTH SENSE?

Though not everyone is ready to acknowledge it, almost everyone does have some curiosity about the metaphysical realms. People tend to describe themselves as 'believing in' or 'not believing in' the realms of the sixth sense. Nevertheless, many of those who insist they are non-believers will sit down happily to listen to an astrologer's or clairvoyant's information about themselves. And there are those who have already some sense of the existence of life beyond the physical realm, but want to find out more by exploring for themselves. Visiting the realm of metaphysics through the *Guide* allows them to do this.

The UK is the land of the Druids and nature worship, Merlin the wizard and of the magical land of Avalon, of the mystical sites of Stonehenge, Avebury and Glastonbury; the traditions go back thousands of years. There has long been interest in these studies. In the current renaissance of interest in metaphysics, London was the site of the first Spiritualist Society, a little over a hundred years ago.

Recently interest has been prompted again by the media. The renewed attention has increased attendance at classes in metaphysical subjects and boosted sales in books as the curious have begun to explore. For many the purpose is in gaining a deeper understanding of how life works. For others, as the world seems to become more orientated to solely physical values or for whom its troubles are disturbing, the metaphysical realm offers a sense of order and a path of greater understanding.

There are a surprising number of people who have had some experiences themselves: precognitive dreams in which what they dreamt later occurred, intuitions in which they had impressions of events to come, sightings of ghosts. If these events occur to the uninformed, they can be frightening, and the recounting of them not necessarily well received by ill-informed friends. Individuals to whom these events have happened want explanations which will relieve the fear and intimidation. Understanding the realm from which these impressions come helps give a better feeling of control over events of this nature and information to use in pursuing any further studies.

BUT I DON'T WANT TO KNOW!

The immediate reaction of a few people to the land of metaphysics, or to one of its kingdoms, is fear or dismissal. Some people are simply not interested in the planes of life beyond the physical. For others the different lands of metaphysics are worrying because they represent things they can't control. For them, if they do decide to explore these realms, it is very important indeed that they be equipped with adequate information so they will not feel intimidated by this new realm with its somewhat strange occupants and curious rules.

WILL I BECOME ONE OF THOSE STRANGE PEOPLE?

It is the view of some that those associated with the metaphysical realm are, well, peculiar. It is an area which attracts strongly individualistic people, and, indeed, a few are peculiar. But so are some professionals, like accountants. And like accountants, many in metaphysics look quite normal. But still there are those who have the impression that while exploring the realm of the sixth sense they will be rubbing shoulders with exceedingly curious people and be thought of as weird themselves. The reality is that, while the clairvoyant in fiction has traditionally been an eccentric, there are many readers and experts in the field who are quite disappointingly normal.

Knowledge provides safe paths for exploration, and reduces the fear of being distracted by any of the kingdom's stranger denizens. Anxieties of this sort come from lack of information, and are perhaps exaggerated by media treatment of some of the metaphysical realm's more outrageous members.

OCCULT WORRIES

The association of metaphysics with the occult is a concern for some. The term occult is unsavoury and unacceptable to some, especially if they are religious. The word actually means 'hidden', and its use in metaphysical areas describes the hidden wisdom and understanding necessary for an individual to comprehend and be able to interpret for others the various realms of the area. For those of a traditional religious orientation, it is worth commenting that the values behind metaphysics are fundamentally spiritual, focusing as they do beyond the physical plane. A large proportion of those drawn to these pursuits have a strong personal faith, often the reason they initially explored studies of this type.

Many of the tools and states of mind used in the metaphysical area may seem a bit strange to those to whom they are new – astrological charts, Tarot cards, people going into trances, for example. But do the instruments used by a doctor look any more familiar, or less intimidating, when first encountered?

You will learn enough in this book to take the strangeness away, and more importantly, gain knowledge enough to be able to judge for yourself.

FINAL DEPARTURE INSTRUCTIONS

From earliest days, you probably have memories of mother waving goodbye as you set off on a journey, calling out, 'Have a good time!' The land of the sixth sense is a land of surprises and delights. It offers information about the present, past and future, amazing sights, and the possibility of finding out about your own psychic skills.

The *Guide* will enable you to do this as an informed traveller, knowing where to go and what to expect, aware of the pitfalls and avoiding them, and being entertained, not taken advantage of, by the charlatans. Most importantly, the understanding of your own world and of the people in it will be broadened by your travels. Many wish to return to the land of metaphysics again and again. Each visit is more enriching and travellers return with wonderful souvenirs, memories and gifts.

2

The Myth of Metaphysics

THE CHOICE: DESTINY OR FREE WILL

Welcome to the land of metaphysics. It is intriguing, exciting, full of new vistas and rich experiences. It also offers a number of choices, some of which will have to be made shortly after arrival.

Just over the border into the realm of the sixth sense, the road forks sharply. A road sign looms above, the old-fashioned sort with hands indicating the different directions. The hand which points one way reads 'Destiny' and the other 'Free will'. The first choice a visitor to this realm will make is which of these paths to follow. Each path leads to a full range of readers representing all of the areas of metaphysical study. The places and readers encountered along the two routes will be quite similar, but there is fundamental difference in the philosophy between the two.

WHAT ABOUT DESTINY?

Select the destiny road, and you enter a world where, for example, the Tarot cards reveal an unchangeable destiny, or the astrologer's horoscope describes the power of the planets over your life. Your choice then lies in planning how to manage with what destiny has dealt out; perhaps you will be forewarned as to when to raise your insurance coverage.

*   *   *

18

There are still many who take this route. Through history this road was by far the more heavily travelled. Most people did not consider that there was much in their lives which could be altered or improved upon. The future seemed fixed. In the 'good old days', the majority of people had to work so hard, men at their jobs, women taking care of and feeding families at home, that very few had the time to think about how to do more than cope with their destiny. The people who had money and the leisure time also had, by and large, comfortable enough lives and so were not usually inclined to wonder much about how to change them.

The destiny route is still the most popular one with those from the Far East, from India, and from the rest of Asia. Perhaps this is because in that part of the world most still have a smaller range of choices about how to live their lives than do those in the West. Elements such as economics, family background and religion still very much limit options available to an individual born in this part of the world. For them the metaphysical realm tells of their unchangeable destiny.

Visitors who choose this path will use the *Guide* to learn how to select the best readers and consultants. Those consultants, and there are some fine ones, who use this approach help show how visitors can get the most out of their destiny. Even though the choice of the path is an important one, as it colours the way all of life is viewed, in the land of metaphysics it is not an irreversible one. Some may choose to try the destiny path for a while on an experimental basis. The option is still available at any time to take the other road, the one which says free will.

FREE WILL FOR YOU?

The free will route follows a road peopled with consultants very like those encountered along the destiny road. There are card readers and astrologers and clairvoyants. The big difference is not what they do; it is the approach they take in doing it. A reader from the free will road will say what the future looks like from the view of the moment of the reading and with the attitude that any situation revealed can be altered. For example, a card reader will tell what is shown in the cards – perhaps, a problem at work. A free-will-orientated reader will explain the matter in terms which will suggest options for its resolution. This may require an inner change on the part of the client, or possibly some sort of discussion with a colleague. Any shift made will then be reflected in the 'fortune'. Those in the free will realm believe that the future is ever unfolding, and if attitudes are changed, the cards, read again even on the same day, will come out differently. Yet if no changes are made the cards read a month later would be very nearly the same.

WHOSE RESPONSIBILITY IS IT?

The next fork in the road has two signs: one says 'Empowering Others', and the other 'Taking Responsibility'. The way along the empowering road looks a little like the destiny road. For those who take this route, every reader is perceived as knowing more than the client. While it is true that some consultants are very expert, empowering them takes away the client's power to evaluate what they say. There are some who do indeed feel that readers and consultants know more about their lives than they do themselves. As an example, someone may go to a past-life regressionist and be told that their partner's wandering eye results from their having been extremely possessive in a past life. While the relationship may be a perfectly happy one, with no signs of strain, those who empower readers will accept this, even though there is no sign of it being applicable. Those who empower readers in this way allow what the reader says to colour their view, and they can worry over matters which aren't really issues at all. As will be said often in this book, even the best readers have blind spots, areas where they will not be able to 'see' accurately.

Empowering readers in this way suspends one's own good sense in favour of another's view. And in the land of metaphysics, it is sometimes tempting and very easy to do.

MAKING YOUR CHOICE

The 'taking responsibility' road requires more effort, because, instead of accepting what a reader says wholesale, statements must be reviewed, considered and evaluated to see how each fits into life. And it is necessary to be willing to speak up and to question.

Doing this with the past-life regressionist would have resulted in a question such as, 'What you said just doesn't seem to fit. Could you tell me more?' It might be revealed that the issue is not really possessiveness, but actually the need for each to spend some time building separate activities. It could equally have been an issue on the part of the reader, projected on to the client.

The metaphysical realm is a very subjective place. Readings are the result of both the skill and the interpretation of the reader. Even the very best and most highly trained readers are human and have their share of problems and their own life lessons to grapple with. Sometimes it is the sensitivity to and awareness of their own life's difficulties which gives them compassion and the ability to work with other people's inner worlds and their issues. And occasionally, especially in untrained or less experienced readers, this same sensitivity makes it more difficult for them to detach themselves sufficiently to interpret information clearly. Often all that's needed to clear up any problem is a question. This is not challenging the skill of the reader, but merely asking for clarification. This prevents empowering the consultant and gets the best from a reading.

DO YOU WANT TO BE RESCUED?

Once the decision's been made about who's going to keep the power in your paranormal experiences, there will be another temptation. Next will appear a huge sign which says, 'YOU GOT IT, WE'LL FIX IT!' There is an enormous striped tent with colourful flags flying and people wandering around the great number of booths set up like a circus sideshow. Those here have cures and remedies for every condition that ails you and for some things you never thought of. And not only for the physical, as this is the realm of the sixth sense! There's a fellow who says if everyone meditates as he tells them to, they will be peaceful all the time. Appealing? And here's someone who says his class in psychic development will enable you to read other people's minds. There are several who say their diet will prevent aging (and every diet is different). And here's a healer who promises that you can get rid of that lower backache without the exercise your doctor's been insisting on. There's never time for the exercise anyway and the healer says that he'll take care of it all.

These promises are very alluring. Many of those offering them seem so serene or accomplished themselves, that it is difficult to imagine they would have any but the highest of motives. Some of them do have high convictions, and many have high opinions of themselves as well! The motivation of others is not quite so pure. Yet many who travel this road are lured here. Some catch on quickly to these metaphysical snake oil salesmen. Others stay on, always seeking the easy remedy to life's problems. Though nothing ever gets completely fixed, there is always something new to try out. They all say their method will take care of everything without the need to make any effort (except, perhaps for paying them . . .) Never is it suggested that examining the cause of the problem will have results.

This sideshow can be the most disillusioning part of a visit to the metaphysical realm. In spite of having decided to be responsible and not empower others, it is still tempting to think there may be someone whose technique would solve life's challenges easily.

Many stop here and sample the wares. It's possible to

learn a great deal and some of the offers made are quite entertaining. Most visitors start with the readers and consultants who have flashy tents, exotic methods and offer quick results. The flamboyant mediums, those who make dramatic predictions with promises of immediate wealth and love, the healers who have instant cures. As their dramatic presentations lose fascination, visitors turn to those who are more complex and subtle, who say their method won't work unless something is given up, or who charge high fees. And some of these are very charming and charismatic. They say everyone can be as happy as they are by doing exactly as they do. And they will show you how – for a price! Others insist on a great deal of study, or extreme practices of meditation, or exercise in pursuit of promised spiritual goals. And they believe it. Some have been seduced by their own talk, and their conviction may carry you for a while. Enjoy it! It's entertaining. And educational. This is the beginning of the process of learning to discriminate in the metaphysical realm. Many of the denizens are very glamorous and offer an amazing variety of services. Once you are able to assess the promises these people make, you will be safe from the seductive side of this realm.

You have seen through the myth of the metaphysical. These distractions lure every new visitor to the kingdom. From time to time there may be another glittering temptation; there are always different versions appearing with new promises. But you'll never again think you need someone else to rescue you. You will know how to consult the very best to get assistance and direction, and how to employ it to your benefit.

3

Now That You're Here, Get to Know the Ropes

Although the individual characteristics of the realms of the metaphysical world are treated in each chapter of the *Guide*, there are fundamental standards, ethics and obligations on the part of readers and practitioners which every visitor should be acquainted with. In the same way, it is the responsibility of the visitor to learn some of the basic laws of the realm being visited. As is the case with a visit to any new country, it's a process of getting acquainted, and it's more fun once you get to know the ropes.

EXPECTATIONS

It is safe to say that no one arrives in the realm of metaphysics without some anticipation of what they will get during their stay. Exactly what those expectations are vary widely with each visitor. Some are looking for readers to answer all their questions, others are hoping that time with a consultant will somehow simply erase life's problems.

To be fair, what visitors expect to get is based on hearsay – stories from friends that can only give a personal impression, and reports in the press and magazines, perhaps not always the most objective or least sensational in their presentation. The wise visitor wants to know about standards, what can reasonably be anticipated from a consultant, what responsibilities they as a client may have and what might be considered to be out of line. While mind reading may be one of the techniques used in the realm of the sixth sense, visitors needn't rely on their intuition and will find their time there more comfortable if they can read in black and white what they may look forward to.

THE READERS' RESPONSIBILITY

In most areas of endeavour, the definition of the term professional is the exchange of fee for service, which incurs certain obligations on the part of each participant. In the realm of metaphysics, it is the exchange of energy alone which creates these obligations. To put this simply, any individual who uses a skill from one of the realms of the sixth sense, whether in a professional setting or not, financially compensated, or not, is still using energy from the realm and is responsible for what they say. In this sense, someone casually reading a palm at a cocktail party has as great an obligation as a highly paid and well-known psychic in a personal appointment with a client.

We must be this rigorous because no exchange of energy from the metaphysical realm is ever frivolous, even if done in the most informal of circumstances. As is the case with doctors, there is a tendency for those untrained in their field to take even their most lightly stated comment very seriously. Experienced readers, and even those who are students, should be mindful of this when they speak. Even a remark made in a humorous vein could well be taken to heart by someone listening.

Equally, when engaged in their craft, be it doing readings of one sort or another or healing, metaphysical consultants have a responsibility to be clear in what they say, state what they can do and what they can't, giving the client realistic expectations of what they will get for their time and money. In a realm as subjective as the metaphysical one, it is not always easy to make absolute statements about what will come from a session, but it is possible to make an estimate, and, if the client asks, it is their right to have one. It is a bit like taking a car in to be repaired − it is not until the mechanic looks at it that he is able to say what may be the matter, and even then he reserves the right to revise his assessment of the work needing to be done. But just as it is his obligation to report on these before doing additional work, so similarly are metaphysical professionals obliged.

Can anyone really tell your fortune? Some visitors and some readers think so. For those who have taken the point of view that their destiny is already written, this would be the expectation. When making an appointment, both the reader and the client should make clear the orientation of the session.

Until visitors have become experienced 'old-timers' in the metaphysical realm, with years of readings to look back on, there remains a dilemma. The difficulty is in understanding how, if readers get some things so right, how are other things they say so wrong? Readings will include past events stated accurately, and present and future ones which may already be unfolding; it is only as time passes that many of what appeared to be accurate predictions do not come to pass. As is explained more thoroughly in the chapter on clairvoyance, this occurs because a reading is a slice through the present, revealing potentials only. The future remains the client's to shape. Some predictions will come to pass with an inevitability which seems almost destined, yet they are only the result of actions in the past. This recognises free will, but points out that some events seem like fate because the ball behind them started rolling so long ago.

The following is a comprehensive list of the responsibilities of those in the field. As it is inclusive, not every point will be applicable to every area. It is the obligation of *all consultants and readers*, even in casual settings, to:

· Make understandable statements in jargon-free language.
· Answer questions directly and clearly.
· State what can and cannot be seen, or accomplished.
· Respect the confidentiality of the client.
· Make no promises which cannot be fulfilled.

26

And for those in professional settings they should also:
- Give answers to questions about background, experience, training, etc.
- Definite statement of fee, duration of session.
- Describe what session will cover.
- Be punctual, and give full uninterrupted attention.
- Provide a quiet place to work.

All of the listed elements reflect an attitude, the core of which is respect: both by the reader, or consultant, and the client. By politely but firmly demanding these conditions, clients are asking for the best, not only of the extraordinary things the metaphysical realm has to offer, but for themselves as well.

CLIENTS' RESPONSIBILITIES AND RIGHTS

While many of the obligations of readers and consultants noted above are shared by the client, the client will derive more benefit from any session or consultation if the following suggestions are noted.

About the session:
- Give some thought to the purpose of the session.
- Realise that a reader can only give so much information.
- Be punctual, pay for appointments missed without cancellation.
- Be honest, do not hide your identity or mis-state the purpose of your visit.
- Be reasonable in letting the reader know what is on your mind.

Realistic expectations:
- Do not expect the reader to make you feel better magically.
- Do not expect a quick solution to major problems.
- Don't blame reader for saying things you don't want to hear.
- Do not expect reader to change the conditions you created in your life.

· Do not try to convince a consultant to do what they say they can't.

Expect to get:
  · Improved understanding of yourself.
  · Clarity on situations.
  · Timetable for events.
  · Better understanding of others.
  · Projection of what will occur if present behaviour goes on unchanged, or suggestion of results of altered behaviour.
  · Explanation of reasons for limits, delays and disappointments in life and suggestions for changing situation.
  · Overview of past, present and future life trends.
  · Clear answers to questions.

About predictions:
  · Understand that readers reveal trends, and sometimes cannot be exact in their predictions.
  · Understand that some predictions may only make sense after the passage of time.
  · Understand that the exercise of personal free will alters the outcome of predictions.
  · Suspect too rosy a prediction.

Protecting yourself:
  · Question statements which don't make sense, or are frightening.
  · Don't expect reader to give guarantees.
  · If a reader suggests returning for more appointments for no reason you can understand, ask why.
  · Do not pay more than agreed beforehand for a session.
  · Beware of broad statements such as 'you will never', you 'have no choice'.

While this book will give both concise information and fascinating tales of the metaphysical realms, the above guidelines may be the most important of what it has to offer. This can be considered to be a master list, though it will be restated several times in the individual chapters, adapted to the characteristics of the various realms.

By remembering and utilising these, both consultants and clients will derive more from their time together, better understand what is expected and be able to live up to the potentials offered for those who explore the extraordinary realm of metaphysics.

4

You're On Your Own – Making a Choice

As a guidebook this is intended to aid and inform as you explore the realms of the sixth sense. It will serve as a bridge across the gulf between the familiar day-to-day world and the metaphysical one, explaining simply and without strange jargon the way this realm functions and introducing its vocabulary. It will not overwhelm with encyclopaedic detail – it will rather give a foundation from which further exploration can take place, remaining an easy reference tool as new complexities are encountered along the way.

There are different ways to explore. You may be an armchair explorer and choose to expand your metaphysical horizons by reading more specialised books after this one has acquainted you with the basic lie of the metaphysical land. This book will give you enough knowledge to know what to ask for next. Or you may be eager to take off and consult readers yourself, take classes, personally experience techniques such as meditation or healing. It will tell you how to find what you're looking for and how to evaluate what you've found. If you are totally new to this area, in addition to familiarising you with the language used, it will help you understand the metaphysical view of the world.

WHY A GUIDE IS NECESSARY

Travel guidebooks are not only an introduction to an area, but give details of the places of interest, and explain the customs of the country. This is important in a place where, for example, the dining habits, mealtimes and the cuisine are completely unfamiliar. In a new country, it is as helpful to understand how to find the way, and knowing about the customs and habits, even more, perhaps, than having specific recommendations. Guidebooks which give specific recommendations become outdated quickly as suggested places change and new ones appear. Good guides tell you how to track down places of interest, assess them, and give suggestions for individual exploration.

The metaphysical realm has a powerful and personal impact on its visitors. Each arrives with their own goals and desires, and discovers more while there. Some come looking for answers to particular questions, for an understanding of life's puzzles, others for treatment or care. Initial visits are often confusing, as it can take some time to discover those who will give the kind of information or treatment desired. Before setting out to search for a consultant, it is useful to know what sort to look for, how to seek them out, and what to expect from them; the *Guide* will help with this process.

FINDING THE BEST

Rather than listing and recommending individual readers and consultants, this book will show you how to find and evaluate them. Once you've acquired the skills for judging the best, seeking them out can be fun. And as the status, quality and availability of readers can change over time, there can be no reliable permanent reference. One becomes well-known, gets busy, fees go up while others appear who are equally as good, just not quite as well known. And it is possible to stumble on someone completely unknown who is wonderfully skilled. Often the undiscovered gem of a reader is a better bet than the one everyone's flocking to.

You may have decided it's time to try meditation, or perhaps to see a healer. The range of quality is as wide as

31

the range of services. If you're just beginning your explorations, the *Guide* will be an aid and give useful standards to apply in the process.

HOW TO FIND A READER

There are numerous resources for finding readers. The first choice is a friend's referral. Assessment of just how sensible the friend is will help judge the worth of the referral. Someone whose life is often in disarray, and has little sense of judgement themselves, is perhaps not the most astute of evaluators. On the other hand, if someone is clear minded and likes to get good value for money, they will have given serious thought to any consultant they have seen and will only recommend someone after due consideration.

Find centres and booksellers specialising in metaphysics in your area. Sometimes staff members give readings. Often at centres there are many types of consultants, ranging from astrologers to past-life readers, healers to mediums, so there will be a variety to try. They often have newsletters, classes, meetings and open days.

There is also a tremendous number of wonderful readers lurking in villages and small towns. Not associated with centres of any sort at all, and perhaps not even formally trained, mother, grandmother and great-grandmother before will all have read the cards, tea leaves or whatever. Often these people are natural counsellors, with a gift that years of study can never bestow. Naturally, not all of these are good. But if you run across one, give them a try, and evaluate the experience using the guidelines in this book. The fee is not normally high and as long as you are careful to assess what is said, the risk is low.

It is also very important to remember that some of the best readers are not popular with everyone. While some build their trade based on pleasing their clientele and telling them pretty much what they want to hear – saying *everything* a client wants to hear would be too suspicious. A rather direct and incisive psychic or astrologer will sometimes tell a client what even their best friends won't say. And often this does not make them popular, in the short run anyway. Like many situations in which home truths are dispersed, the reason and usefulness of them is seen later. So it is with readers. The 'pleasers' will be regarded favourably for a week or so, then forgotten, like a quickly swallowed sweet. The more straightforward readers will leave a stronger and more lasting impression.

The choice of the type of reader really depends on the needs of the moment. Sometimes the reason for consulting a reader is the need for a quick overview, or perhaps, if you're a bit down, for affirmation that things will, indeed, turn out all right. The more gentle, positive, less-challenging reader is the sort for those moments. But if it's time to come to grips with a situation, or major life changes are under consideration and another view seems appropriate, then the more incisive reader is needed.

WHAT SPECIALITY OF READER TO SEE?

The first step is to take a moment, sit down and focus on exactly what kind of information and what degree of detail is desired. This will influence the type of reader. There is quite a range in readings. An astrologer will be more precise about timing and will often give an excellent profile of the nature of any situation at hand and what is unfolding in it. A psychic will rather come up with the breathtaking facts about the present and the future, but can sometimes be considerably off beam in matters of timing. In other words, an astrologer is more likely to be able to tell you the *date* you will meet the love of your life, but a psychic or clairvoyant will be able to tell you what they will look like, perhaps even the colour they will be wearing, yet may be a year out on the date!

If the matter at hand is the launching of a new business and the aim is to get things off to a well-timed start, then it is likely an astrologer or a numerologist will fill your requirements for a fairly exact timetable for the next couple of months. But if there is a very complicated situation with personalities and politics at work and the need is to get a overall picture, a clairvoyant will be more able to give intuitive information on the people and suggestions for how to handle it.

As a general rule, for greater exactitude in time and general accuracy, the more mechanistic methods of reading are the best choice: astrology, numerology, to a certain extent palmistry. For more generic information with greater detail, but with less overall accuracy, consult one of the more intuitive disciplines: a psychic or clairvoyant, a Tarot or card reader, a medium.

WHERE DO READERS COME FROM?

Professional readers in any of the metaphysical fields are often asked how they got into that line of work. It is a safe bet that when they were little children and asked what they wanted to be when they grew up, very few of them said they'd like to be a clairvoyant! Career counsellors generally do not list this field in their selection of vocations; so those who have made their way to this area, especially if they are full-time professionals, have had to make the journey on their own. It makes for a field full of strong individuals.

The consultant in the metaphysical field, be it clairvoyant, astrologer, healer or palmist, tends to be portrayed as eccentric, sometimes accurately. Two types are most prominent: the Margaret-Rutherford-as-Madame-Arcati image – the scatty medium with fringed shawl flying behind her from the Noel Coward comedy *Blithe Spirit* – and the left-over hippie with lank hair, an Afghan jacket, toting a crystal.

First-time visitors to some consultants are disappointed. Expecting to see someone outrageous and colourful, they are greeted by a perfectly ordinary conventionally groomed person. Oh, perhaps you will run into the odd Madame Arcati, and a few hippies, but this is not the norm. In fact in recent years interest in the metaphysical realm has grown amongst professionals, and there is an increasing number of them who have come to study and work in this area, bringing their polish and businesslike quality with them.

ARE READERS SPECIAL PEOPLE?

One might equally ask are doctors special people? The answer is a firm yes and no. Yes, they are special because they have taken the time to find a speciality in an area as yet regarded as unusual, and to hone a skill in it. As is the case with many of the professions, most readers will have spent some years of their lives studying in order to be able to do what they do.

What probably makes readers most special is that they have chosen to share their skill with others. As becoming a reader in the metaphysical is not the most common career choice, it takes a special nature and a particular concern for others to enter the field. And this does make most of the people you will encounter warmer and more caring than the usual.

CAN YOU TRUST YOUR READER?

Most often a first visit to a reader is occasioned by a crisis. Not many go to readers for pure amusement. So while you may feel a little awkward sharing information with a reader about delicate and possibly intimate matters, remember, a reader is rather like a doctor – they hear it all day. As difficult as what you are discussing may be, the reader has probably dealt with that sort of thing before.

Readers, especially those who make their living as consultants, are interested in keeping their clientele. So you can assume that any very personal matters you share with them will be in safe hands. An indiscreet reader quickly loses his custom. Readers, because they have heard it all, are often pretty good at being practical agony aunts as well as utilising their specific area of expertise, so you may benefit from your reader's handling of previous clients' problems too!

THE FRINGE ELEMENT

Speaking of fringes, it is important to mention the minority in the field – the weirdos. They are, unfortunately, often the most visible: 'witches' with masses of black eye-makeup; clairvoyants who allude to 'knowing' something about you and then won't tell what it is.

There are two types of peculiar we are talking about here. The first is relatively innocent and yet is the most obvious. There is the oddly got-up individual who looks a bit like a caricature from a play doing the part of, well, a weird person from the metaphysical realm. They are usually pretty harmless, and sometimes quite skilled as readers, so it may take time to see if the eccentricity is just that.

The second type stands out less, and in fact on first meeting may seem very polished and charming. There is just one tiny flaw. Their knowledge is a power trip for them. They use metaphysical techniques to take advantage of others. These readers can do great harm. They are the manipulators and con men of metaphysics. An example would be a psychic who implies he knows something important about you and then won't tell what it is. This is a characteristic of this sort of reader: the technique of manipulation, the withholding of information, designed to keep you nervous and coming back. The range of exact techniques varies with the specific field. If any reader says you *must* come back for more work, that you have a curse on you which the reader can fix, that you *must* buy protection, lessons, or anything which is costly, just leave. If you are threatened, for example, with a statement such as, 'If you do not do as I suggest, there may be undesirable results,' leave and call the police. Do not be embarrassed, or think what you have to say is unimportant, as you may have been one of many who have been similarly manipulated, and may be of help in their investigations. Unfortunately, there is fraud in the field of metaphysics as elsewhere. It is a tiny proportion, but because there is very little in the way of regulation or licensing in the area, it falls to alert consumers to take both notice and action.

HOW TO PREPARE FOR YOUR VISIT TO A READER

There is probably already something specific on your mind as the main topic for a reading. It may be a need to get direction in a certain area of life, or it may be a clear turning point. It is worth while to take a few moments to think if there are any related issues to explore with the main topic. Readings can be about anything of concern: personal life such as family, relationships, your partner, children, friends, work and your livelihood, career, health, money, hobbies, understanding the past better and preparing for the future.

For example, there may be an offer of a job promotion with a relocation. Not only will it be important to know how this will affect your career, but also any relationships in your life – obviously, if you're married, your partner, but possibly other family members and friends as well. Even anxieties that can't quite be pinned down can be dealt with, often rather well, in sessions of this type.

Always ask if you can tape-record your session. Readers vary widely in their feelings on this matter. Some actually prefer it themselves, others find it makes them uncomfortable. If you cannot tape your session, take enough paper to make thorough notes. No matter how you try, it is not possible to remember everything said. The mind plays very funny tricks and often quickly remodels some of the information into something easier to accept. For this reason, go over the notes from the reading immediately after the session, before discussing it with anyone else, and flesh out what you've written during the reading even further.

Then take a moment to evaluate how you felt about what was said. No matter what kind of reading it was, only you can determine if it was constructive. This is a subjective process and takes judgement. Sometimes information given may not be pleasing to hear at first! Yet even though what was said may not have fallen in line with your fantasies, does it seem that it was in your best interests, and was it life-affirming? Did the reader seem to be on your side? All of these impressions will help the process of weighing how much to rely on the information given. It is your choice. In some cases a clear picture may not be easily seen and it may take a few months before you are able to decide how you feel about the reading.

Only after this is done is it time to consider sharing the information in the reading with friends. As close and as loving as friends may be, they have their own view of you and of their desires for you. A very good friend might unconsciously be discouraging about making that job move because of fear of losing a valued companion. On the other hand, if you're having difficulty in seeing the sense of something you were told in a reading, a friend may be able to help rationalise that element of the reading.

Often things will be said in a session, especially if it is very orientated to prediction of the future, which simply don't seem possible. You just can't imagine how it will happen. Readings are about the future, and though every reading will have some predictions which simply never come to be, there will be others which will only make sense or seem possible when some other event happens first. Don't reject out of hand the possibility of an appealing but seemingly impossible prediction coming to pass. By becoming more experienced at this sort of 'future-viewing', you will develop a reasonable intuition for seeing what of the 'unlikely' may be likely.

EXPLORING THE BOOK

Each chapter of the *Guide* is a self-contained unit about one area of the land of metaphysics. Those who read the book straight through, rather than going directly to the chapter on their area of interest, will notice some repetition. For those who miss it by skipping the introductory chapters, very important information is repeated in every relevant chapter.

After describing the nature of each realm, each chapter will give information about:

- What it is.
- How it is done.
- What you can expect to experience there and derive from it, and what you can't.
- Who does it, how they would typically have learned how to do it, and how to evaluate them.
- How and where to find them.
- What are the likely costs and how often you might go to see them.
- Tales of real-life visitors.
- Warning signs.
- How to explore on your own, to study, and some things you can do yourself.

PACKING FOR YOUR TRIP

You're off on an amazing trip. Take your curiosity, and an enquiring mind. Take your common sense. And most important, take your sense of wonder. This is a land beyond the 'practical' limitations of the day-to-day. It transcends the concrete world, probing back into time, forward into tomorrow's possibilities and altering the present through transformational methods. When most visitors leave, they discover they have a wonderful souvenir to take home with them − the vision of a world of wider dimensions.

5

You Want to Do It Yourself

After the initial get-acquainted visits to the metaphysical realm, newly sophisticated explorers have some choices. Depending on your degree of interest and involvement, there are several paths open. Some are content with continuing to make visits from time to time, perhaps expanding the range of consultants they see. Others will be ready to take a deeper look into the realm and what it offers in terms of personal exploration. For a few, the metaphysical will have become a sufficient source of interest and gratification that they consider the possibility of becoming a practitioner.

For serious students the metaphysical realm will be a resource, a place to consult with experts, to get a view about themselves and their life, and to be treated. For them, visits to now-familiar consultants and readers will continue to make up the majority of their time spent there. There may be occasional explorations into new territories, to see what may be derived from them.

DEEPER STUDY

After getting well acquainted with the various areas, some explorers will be ready for deeper study. They will be ready to use metaphysical techniques for more intense personal development. Rather than see consultants from time to time for just a 'check up', visits will be more frequent and the aim will be to delve into matters requiring focused attention. For example, instead of simply hearing about previous lives from a past-life regressionist, work will be done to understand their effects and if necessary reduce these in this incarnation.

The interests of others will be focused beyond solely personal concerns into study of the methods behind the practices used in the different realms, and deeper understanding of their philosophies. The next steps include a variety of options, amongst these are attending lectures, courses and events such as weekend workshops, or undertaking to become an individual student.

For those interested, there is no lack of choice of courses, workshops and seminars. At first these are a little difficult to find; groups offering them rarely advertise much. The best way to learn about what is available is by 'networking', that is making further contacts with those with shared interests. All you have to do to get into that network is ask questions. Connections come from meeting with and talking to others. New centres and study groups appear regularly and they offer more and more events. So an authoritative list of shops, centres or consultants quickly becomes out of date.

Many organisations have mailing lists and send announcements of programmes or have newsletters showing schedules. It could be said that nearly every weekend there is some sort of workshop, class, seminar or other metaphysically orientated event, so once the connection is made, there is no dearth of choice.

Exploring in this way also offers the opportunity to meet others who are similarly interested. Many who have been intrigued with the field but have not had anyone to talk with are delighted finally to discover a world of people who love to exchange thoughts about metaphysical ideas.

BECOMING A CONSULTANT

Some become so interested and find the area rewarding enough to want to become a consultant. The next steps vary with the type of speciality. Astrology attracts many – there are courses available to attend or to do by correspondence. If mediumship or spiritualism is the focus, the Spiritualist Society offers classes. While not all areas of the metaphysical world fly banners about the instruction available, every aspect has those who teach as well as practise. Some keep a very low profile because they do not especially want members of the general public coming for tuition, only those who have a committed interest and are willing to show it by doing a bit of digging to find the classes. But it is worth the investigation. The mastery of skills in the metaphysical realm requires personal supervision, especially if the goal is becoming a consultant. There are some things that just can't be learned from books.

As with all aspects of the realm, the number of places to study and be trained are growing, and there are so many new ones, it is impossible to keep up with them. Of course, there are the old, traditional centres of study and training. Anyone who is seriously wishing to study would be well advised to take the time to enquire further. There is a good chance of discovering a new faculty, a new centre, or a course which suits your interests perfectly. And there is the value in meeting people in the process of the search as well.

For those who do not live near major cities, or are in places where the interest in metaphysics has not yet resulted in centres or bookshops, there is no need to feel cut off. At first a trip into a town for some research may be required, or at the least a bit of telephoning. The goal is to find a shop or centre which either has a correspondence course or will let you know about new publications as they become available. It's a matter of getting into the 'network' again.

If considering joining a course, enquire thoroughly about it. This is important not only for the obvious reason of avoiding getting involved in something that is not what it seems to be, but also to make sure the style of teaching and the content of the course suits your needs. Ask to speak to a graduate, and enquire of them how much they use the information they learned, how helpful the instructors were, and in general if they can recommend the course to you. Naturally, be suspicious of courses which cannot produce any graduates for you to speak to!

TECHNIQUES TO TRY OUT

Not everyone will want to do courses or study. Some people like to try things out themselves; for them the next step is experimentation. There are a few areas of the metaphysical realm safe for even a beginner. While some are too complicated, take a long time to learn, or bear too great a responsibility with them, the following may provide a good introduction for those who wish to experiment on their own.

Tarot or Playing Cards

The only equipment necessary is a deck of cards and a manual. And lots of friends willing to wait while you look up what each card means in the book. It is slow and painstaking at first, but many get the knack of reading cards very quickly. The more you practise, the easier it gets. Some find Tarot cards easier to read as they have pictures on them which symbolise their meaning; others have a natural leaning to using playing cards.

Tea Leaves

Though instruction books do exist for reading tea leaves, the talent seems to be inborn. The ability to see forms suggestive of events from a spread of scattered leaves is a display of true intuition. Aside from using a book to learn how to brew the leaves properly, how to select tea of the right texture and an ideally shaped cup, practice is the great teacher here.

Astrology, Numerology, Palmistry

Fascinating fields, any student who lets it be known that he is even remotely expert in these will find great popularity at a party. A queue will quickly form for readings. If your background is having read only a few books, then you may be on thin ice, as there are an amazing number who have read widely themselves on these topics and may know more than you. If you are actually a student, and someone asks for a reading, give it a go. No matter how insecure you feel, there are those willing to listen! And it is good practice.

WORDS OF WARNING

No matter what the field of interest is, there are a few guidelines which the beginner had best observe when doing readings. Until the combination of experience and greater knowledge provides one's own inner sense of what is appropriate, these will suffice:

- Never make broad statements to others such as 'you will never', 'you cannot', or 'you must'. Do not speak of a major loss of any type or of the death of the person you are reading or of anyone near to them. You may be taken more seriously than you think.
- Never press someone to give them information or a reading. If you offer, do so in a way which makes it easy for them to decline.
- Do not give advice, just say your view of the situation.
- Don't be funny; your humour may be taken literally.
- Be sensitive to other's personal idiosyncrasies and fears.
- Learn from the people you work with; ask how accurate you have been and how well you have expressed yourself.
- Until you are properly trained, do not take on anyone who appears to be deeply troubled or has had a recent trauma.

AREAS NOT TO BE EXPERIMENTED WITH

While it is possible to view many of the aspects of metaphysics in a light manner, there are some which are simply not for play. One of these areas is best never done without training, the other only with care. Both these areas require proficiency, knowledge of how to protect oneself and others, and experience.

Spiritualism, Channelling, Automatic Writing, Ouija Boards

All of these invite another energy or being into your energy field and mind. Until you know how to control the level of energy being received, and how to make sure that the being leaves when the session is over, this area is definitely no nonsense. Even the 'innocent' Ouija board can bring very peculiar and sometimes frightening results from unwise experimentation, as many who played with one in their teens can attest.

Healing

The reason for care with this is more subtle. It is necessary clearly to discern the purpose of the healing and the needs of the subject. It is reasonable to say that any mother who soothes a sick child's brow is sending out healing energy, and nothing could be safer and more wonderful than that. Then what could be dangerous in healing? In the case of individuals who are very ill, or whose disease has a serious psychological aspect, the energies are too complicated for the novice student to tackle. Unless you know how to clear yourself of the energy of the person healed, they can end up feeling terrific, and you will experience their symptoms. While you're unlikely to develop anything as extreme as a medical condition from healing another, it still is wise to wait until the technique of putting up a protective shield has been learned.

Keep 'practice' healing to simple cases such as injuries from sport and the odd headache.

METAPHYSICAL CHAT

Some find it surprising how many are truly interested in the metaphysical realm. While the number who will go see a consultant or reader from time to time is large, those who are interested are probably triple that, as anyone who has brought up the topic in a social setting has found out.

Enthusiastic students do need one warning, however. It is very easy to do harm to the image of the field by zealously presenting information as if it were the answer to all humankind's ills. The metaphysical realm does offer helpful and penetrating answers to personal issues and some valuable views on world issues as well. It does not have the answer to everything, however, and those who present it in that light will be likely to be seen as off-puttingly pushy rather than helpful. Not everyone has a personality which inclines them to an interest in the metaphysical world, and no amount of talking will make it so. In social situations the best policy is 'inform, don't try to convince'.

If, as a student, you are questioned, be simple in your responses. Try not to use jargon, but speak as directly as possible. Don't give a lecture, nor try to sell the listener on metaphysical thought. Reply as best you can, but if you do not know the answer to a question, say so. In the metaphysical field no one ever knows all the answers! Professionals can be well warned to temper their enthusiasm. Those in the field sometimes overwhelm with a dose of information which gives the listener metaphysical indigestion, often forgetting that most people live and work in a less philosophically orientated world. Small portions of ideas are more likely to be well received.

BON VOYAGE!

Further travels on the metaphysical road promise a wondrous journey. Every turning presents a new vista of awareness, new understanding of self and of others. The goal of the realm is to bring inner peace through union of the spirit, mind and body. Some philosophers believe every step each individual takes in that direction equally advances all those with whom he shares humanity.

Welcome to the realm of metaphysics! Enjoy your explorations!

PART TWO

The Guide

6

Astrological Surprise

Today, astrology is not only familiar, it seems inescapable.
Magazines, newspapers, radio and television all feature it.
From time to time everyone takes a peek at one of the
many astrological columns in magazines and newspapers –
especially newspapers. Daily, weekly and monthly predictions of what is going to happen for each star sign appear,
and these columns have become a vital feature of newspapers. Because of this most newcomers to the metaphysical
realm already know the basics of astrology, that it uses the
zodiac, which is divided into the twelve star signs, that
the birthdate determines an individual's star sign, and that
each sign has particular traits of character, personality and
habits, likes and dislikes.

For those who wish to explore further, there is a wealth
of reading material. There are astrological books describing
each individual star sign in greater depth than is possible
in magazines or newspaper columns, and a variety of
annual zodiac prediction books, which tell in detail what
the coming year holds for each sign, as well as magazines
which specialise in astrology.

WHAT'S POP ASTROLOGY?

A surprising discovery for those who do read further is
that there is considerably more to astrology than at first
appears from what is seen in the majority of publications.

When most people refer to astrology, popular astrology

is what they have in mind. The basis of popular astrology and the form in which almost all astrology appears in media is the star sign, which divides the world into twelve groups, as dictated by the birthdate.

Popular astrology is based on the twelve fundamental types of energies depicted by the signs of the zodiac. These energy types are generalisations, but remarkably valid ones, which have evolved over thousands of years of study and observation. When a sign is discussed in popular astrology, or two signs are compared, it is like comparing individuals who have different ways of life. An example would be comparing city dwellers, who will have great similarities, but, of course, would not be exactly alike, with those who live in the country. The city folk may tend to talk faster, be more impatient, less likely to stop and pass the time of day than, for example, would those from the country, whose life is slower paced. The country folk will not be identical either, but will share a manner unlike that of the city dwellers. In the same way pop astrology divides groups of people into what might be called 'energy types', the signs of the zodiac, and identifies the similar qualities of character, tastes, and interests each will have. Pop astrology is fine for studying individuals as types or members of groups. It can be astonishingly accurate when used in this way. But just as discussing 'city folk' or 'country folk' as a group will not give a precise picture of any one individual in that group, so popular astrology cannot give a deep understanding of any one person. What it can do is help in understanding the general outlook that another individual has, and how it will be similar to and different from another's.

Yet from the sheer volume of material available on star sign astrology, ranging from books on all the twelve signs and their characteristics, and those which focus on the analysis of each individual sign, to the ones which make predictions of the future, it would seem astrology has plenty to offer. And there is considerably more: consulting astrology.

CONSULTING ASTROLOGY

Popular astrology is general and deals with groups; consulting astrology is personal in its orientation. Consulting astrology is most frequently conducted by private appointment with an astrologer. As this focuses on the individual and the horoscope rather than the star signs, greater depth of interpretation and much more detail in prediction is possible.

There is an enormous difference between popular astrology and consulting astrology. Though these two branches use the same twelve signs of the zodiac and the planets as a foundation, the way in which they are used diverges considerably from there. A good way of illustrating the difference between the two is to compare them to a medical or psychological advice column in the newspaper and the individual service offered by a medical consultant or psychologist. While you may read advice given in the newspaper, and may even find some of it personally applicable, you also are aware that for a personal concern individual diagnosis or counselling is available. While many do not realise it, parallel options exist between pop astrology and consulting astrology.

In consulting astrology, the chart or horoscope (the terms are interchangeable) is the starting point. The most common is for the birth of an individual, called a natal chart, but event charts are also plotted, for example for the time of the incorporation of a company or the laying of a cornerstone for a building. No matter what the chart is for, it is an astronomically accurate map of the heavens, showing the positions of the signs of the zodiac and of the planets. The calculations necessary are complicated and precise. Fortunately computers can now do the job quickly and accurately. Though there are programs to cast charts, computers are not yet quite up to interpretation of these charts and this task is best left to a live astrologer. Chart interpretation indicates the fundamental nature of the individual – or company – in question. Forecasting is done primarily by comparing the positions of the planets in the original horoscope with those for the time in question.

Basic chart interpretation describes an individual's character, but astrologers can also use charts to analyse the past and predict the future; two individuals' charts can be combined to create a chart of a relationship, and for the commercially orientated, a chart can even be done for a company. And for those whose interest goes further, there is a vast array of techniques and methods on offer. There are also other branches of consulting astrology with specialities ranging from nutrition, the weather, politics, the financial markets, sports, to medicine and psychology.

WHERE ASTROLOGY CAME FROM

Astrology has been used over thousands of years. Through experience, astrologers have developed and refined a tradition of interpretation of the basic elements: the twelve signs of the zodiac, the planets and the horoscope. Whether writing about star signs for newspapers or practising as consultants, they all draw from this ancient knowledge. And though each brings their own individual style to their writing or consultations, the information is derived from the same foundation and uses essentially the same techniques. Each sign is viewed as representing a specific kind of energy, each planet a force of a characteristic type, and as the planets travel through the zodiac, they bring a type change or energy change to the various areas of life. The objective in studying these changes is to gain knowledge in order to increase self-awareness, to better understand others, to improve relationships, to learn about life's cycles and the best time for major moves.

The study of astrology began when mankind started to settle in one location, living by farming lands rather than by nomadic hunting. There being no city lights then, more stars were visible and star-watching was the regular night's entertainment. In the clear skies where mankind's first settlements were located, the stars formed glittering patterns which were seen to have the shapes of animals, objects and people. These are the constellations, which to our eyes are often difficult to recognise. Others, such as the Plough, or, in the Southern Hemisphere, the Southern Cross, everyone learns to spot as a child. Today, for many, air pollution and bright city lights make it difficult to see even these, so it is not easy for us to visualise the starry images our ancestors could see each night.

As, over the generations, the lore of these constellations was taught, myths and tales of the images seen developed: dramas of heroism, conquest, rescue and tragedy. Stretched across the middle of the heavens, running from east to west, is a particular belt of constellations called the zodiac. In this belt are an assortment of figures of animals (Ram, Bull, Crab, etc.), of people and things (a Virgin, a set of scales). This was particularly important because it was across this region of the constellations that the moon and the planets travelled. The ancients observed their progress, whose positions changed nightly, against the unchanging positions of the stars in the night sky. The patterns of movement were recorded over centuries, as were the events which occurred as the planets formed certain relationships in the signs of the zodiac. The study of the position of the signs, the movement of the planets and what happened as they changed was the beginning of the study of astrology. The word 'astrology' actually means 'the study of the stars'. Astronomy, with which it is often confused, means 'the naming of the stars' and is the scientific study of the actual bodies in the heavens, the planets, the stars and other universes.

Knowledge of the seasons of the year was vital in ancient times because it was necessary to know the proper time to plant crops and many rivers flooded seasonally. Getting the timing wrong could mean no food next season. In those times astrology and astronomy were combined and used to foretell times of flooding, knowledge vital to survival. Astrology was first used in ancient Egypt to predict the Nile's floods, as was also the case in neighbouring

Mesopotamia, home of the Sumerians and later the Chaldeans.

Priests used astrology not only to predict the floods, but the fate of rulers and wars as well. Eventually this became a very sophisticated practice, and tradition has it that the Three Wise Men, or Magi, in the story of the birth of Christ, were Chaldean astrologers who had seen the new Messiah in their charts. During this period in history, astrology offered little to the common man. One exception was its practice in the Mayan Indian culture in ancient Mexico, where horoscopes were available to all from astrologers. The Chinese used astrology from 2000 BC, particularly focusing on the season, even making moves in their palaces according to them.

No matter what part of the world, a seasonal calendar was observed, often with festivals noting the transition from one season to another. The year was counted from the days which form the four 'corners' of the year, the longest and the shortest days, the solstices, and the two days in which night and day are completely equal in length, the equinoxes. Understandably, then, knowing when the first day of spring would occur was extremely important. On that day, as the sun rose, the stars of the constellation of Aries faded behind the sun. This is the reason that the first day of the sign of Aries coincides with the first day of spring.

Equally, on the dawn of the longest day of the year the stars of the constellation of Cancer were there behind the rising sun. So the sun was, literally, in the sign of Cancer, the first day of the sign being the first day of summer. Similarly, in the autumn, the sun was in the sign of Libra, and in the winter, the sign of Capricorn.

ASTROLOGICAL IDENTITY CRISIS

Star signs, signs of the zodiac, birth signs are all different ways of saying the same thing. The year is divided up into twelve periods, and according to the date of birth, everyone is in one of these twelve. Everyone that is, except for those whose births are at the very end of one sign and beginning of the next. These people have a 'star sign identity crisis'. If you are uncertain which sign you are, it is difficult to explore further until you know which signs to read. Some born between two signs, sometimes called 'on the cusp' — which literally means on the edge — resort to reading both signs and trying to figure out which is a more accurate representation of their character.

Dates of Astrological Signs for the Twentieth Century	
ARIES	March 20, 21
TAURUS	April 19, 20, 21
GEMINI	May 20, 21, 22
CANCER	June 21, 22
LEO	July 22, 23, 24
VIRGO	August 22, 23, 24
LIBRA	September 22, 23, 24
SCORPIO	October 23, 24
SAGITTARIUS	November 22, 23
CAPRICORN	December 21, 22
AQUARIUS	January 20, 21
PISCES	February 18, 19

The situation is not helped by books and magazines giving slightly different dates as the beginning of each of the signs. With Aries, for example, 21st March will be listed as the beginning date in one publication, but another will say the 22nd. The variation is the same with all the signs. This is because, from one year to another, the signs actually do begin on different dates. Since the beginning of Aries coincides with the first day of spring, there is a specific hour and minute when spring begins, and that time and date varies from year to year by a day or, sometimes, two. Usually there is an item in the newspaper on that day which gives the exact time the new season begins. And the starting dates and hours of the next signs follow in order. There is actually no such thing as 'being on the cusp', as each star sign does have an exact moment of beginning and ending each year.

For those born right on the edge of the signs, the good news is it is possible to find out the date and hour each sign began in a specific year and so discover one's true star sign. It is necessary, however, to know the birth time as exactly as possible (four minutes can make a difference), and calculations will have to be done by an expert such as an astrologer or by an astrological computing service.

NEW TWIST TO OLD SCIENCE

Even though astrology has been around for nearly forever, popular astrology is actually a contemporary twist. Throughout history astrology has been used most by people who had power and money. Far back into ancient times, kings often had court astrologers. The Roman Emperor Augustus I fulfilled the predictions that the astrologer Nigidius made at his birth, that he would rule the world. Pleased with both the prediction and its correct outcome, Augustus had coins issued graced by his birth sign of Capricorn. While the use of astrology remained mainly the prerogative of people in positions of power, who were the only ones who had much in the way of choice in their lives, all Romans could have their horoscope done.

But until recently most humble folk didn't even know the day of their birth, but even if they did, they could do little with the information an astrologer could give them except await the destiny predicted for them. In the Middle Ages and in the Renaissance astrology had other applications. Professionals such as medical doctors used the temperamental type as depicted by astrology to diagnose and treat illness. Astrology was considered a necessary part of education in the Middle Ages; for example, the University of Bologna had a chair of astrology founded in 1125, and it was taught at Cambridge from 1250. There are frequent astrological references in works ranging from Dante's *Divine Comedy*, Chaucer, the plays of Elizabethan England, including those of Webster and, of course, Shakespeare.

Overlapping this flourishing of astrology in culture and literature was a time of scientific exploration. Copernicus published his revolutionary theory that the earth circled the sun, rather than the reverse, as previously thought, in 1543, and at first received a hostile reaction from the Church. A hundred years later, Galileo met the same response. Though the idea of a solar-centred universe was accepted only slowly, when it finally was, it did much to diminish the reputation of astrology as a science, since astrological theory had been based on the premise of the sun, moon and planets orbiting the earth. This set the scene for several centuries of not always dignified debate as to the validity of astrology.

The year 1795 brought the beginning of the popular astrological press to England, with the publication of journals written by astrologers known as 'Zadkiel' and 'Raphael'. Meant strictly for the unquestioning readers, popular publications of this type have continued until today. But it was not until this century that the star sign column appeared. The first columns were printed in the 1920s in England, when astrologer Phillip Naylor began writing a column which continued to his death, then to be taken up by his wife, Phyllis Naylor.

Columns in newspapers and magazines are all considered pop astrology. Their quality ranges enormously. Some are for entertainment purposes only, and most definitely not to be taken seriously, especially some of the daily newspaper columns. It is very difficult to get much depth of prediction in three or four lines in a column which appears daily. While it might be uncannily accurate on the odd day, if it is observed over time, the average will not be impressive. Some fine astrologers try to do it, but their best work will never be found in these columns. Daily newspaper columns are the most unreliable form of astrology and are least representative of its potential for giving precise information; those appearing with weekly and monthly predictions will be better.

Magazine columns have a far wider range of accuracy and of integrity. You will find some of these are written by very good astrologers who put the best of their knowledge into popular astrology's star sign format. Probably the most famous and the most impressive in his accuracy is England's Patric Walker. His columns appear world wide in a range of magazines and newspapers including, in England, *Harpers and Queen*, as Celeste, the *Evening Standard*, and the *Mail*. The predictions Patric Walker makes are always couched in terms of opportunities to be taken advantage of and issues to be dealt with. That is, he, like most modern astrologers today, recognises that we each have to use our own resources to take advantage of times that are opportune, and employ our energies to overcome obstacles. For example, in one of his columns he noted that, for a particular star sign, changes and progress in an important project would occur, but for aims to be achieved, things would have to be better organised on the home front. This is typical of his kind of astrological approach, because it describes the nature of the time and its potential, and still indicates what effort has to be made to allow these potentials to come to fruition.

HOW TO JUDGE A MAGAZINE COLUMN

Some people turn to the astrology column immediately when picking up a magazine, others just glance at them while thumbing through. As appealing as these columns are to read, it's hard to know just how reliable the predictions are. Some take them very seriously, worrying if things don't sound so good, cheered if they do. While it is not wise to rely totally on any general predictions, these columns can give useful pointers and practical warnings about how the future could shape up.

But as there are so many columns and so many predictions,

it is hard to know how to evaluate them. Probably the best way is to make note of how many absolute statements are made in the column. Because these columns are at best only guidelines, a bold 'you will never', or 'you must', is not likely to apply accurately to the one twelfth of the world who shares your sign of the zodiac. Popular or sun sign astrology deals with groups of people, the cycles they are experiencing and how they are likely to react to those cycles. But it is vital to remember that each individual will react to his or her own way.

Ideally, a column will not give rigid predictions, but will suggest a theme for the month for each sign, the areas of life needing attention, and will also give the dates when it is best to take action or to wait. It should also take into account the likely reaction of the character of each star sign to situations predicted. Look for these elements in any column. The ones which leave latitude for the reader's free will are probably more 'accurate' in that they won't try to predict absolutely everything that will happen, but focus instead on the circumstances which will create the possibilities for the events to occur.

It is worth remembering as well that columns are written to focus on the interests of the readership of the magazine or newspaper they appear in. For example, the columns appearing in publications aimed at single working women will not be of any more than general use to a mother of four, whose interests would be considerably different.

YEAR BY YEAR

Quite a few of the astrological columnists also write year-end prediction books. These come in formats ranging from tiny pocket books to coffee-table size. As with all popular astrology, the range of quality is as wide as the selection of sizes the books come in. These books foretell what the coming year holds. Some do it month by month, some week by week, and some even go as far as day by day. The latter is a risky proposition, as free will often interferes with

61

predictions which try to be too precise and, as mentioned before, it is nearly impossible to make predictions which will apply accurately to all ways of living and walks of life. You will have to decide if these books have any use beyond entertainment value by employing the same yardstick for evaluation as with the sun sign columns. Note how fixed their predictions are, or how much they allow for the free will of the individual. Before investing more than a small sum in one of these you also need to ask if this book is likely to be used throughout the whole year.

A WHOLE MAGAZINE FULL OF ASTROLOGY!

The major popular astrological magazines published today try to bridge the large gap between readers who are interested in astrology but are not expert enough to read the symbols in a chart, and those who are very experienced and knowledgeable. This makes for a magazine which has to stretch very wide, so not every article is of interest to every reader. The editors try to put together a range of articles to satisfy every level of knowledge. They cover a very wide assortment of astrological topics, from the horoscopes of famous people to the charts of towns, astrological stock market analysis, readers' questions which are answered using their natal horoscopes, articles for those more sophisticated in terminology on new techniques, plus the usual star sign predictions for each month. Sometimes these publications miss the mark, but often they have articles which are educational and informative so they are worth a look if you want to read more about astrology. Most important, they make an effort, at least editorially, both to make clear what can be done with astrology and to avoid making claims which are extreme.

COMPUTERISED PERFECTION?

Computers appeared on the popular astrological scene in about 1975. They have been a tremendous help and a horror at the same time. Computers are perfect for calculating charts, as a chart, or horoscope, is nothing more than a map of the heavens for a moment in time from the point of view of a specific place on the earth. Through history, part of the professional astrologer's training has included becoming expert at doing these calculations, but the mathematics are complicated and time consuming, and computers can do them faster and more precisely than a very skilled astrologer. Now horoscopes are available, with an optional interpretation, by post from any of a number of computer services. Many of these advertise in magazines and some also have locations in department stores or high-street shopping areas.

A computer-generated reading can seem good value, and it would appear nothing could be better than having a computer work the chart out itself, yet this may not be so. If a computerised interpretation accompanied the chart, it can be amazingly correct in some ways and astonishingly wrong in others. If computers are so good at mathematical calculations, how could this be? While the horoscope produced is very scientific, it takes training to understand and interpret the symbols for the signs and planets which appear in a chart. Though the profiles given with these charts are written by professional astrologers, a computer cannot yet adequately synthesise the information derived from the position of each planet in each sign and area of the chart to give a clear and accurate astrological profile.

While it's a good idea to have the chart itself calculated by a computer (and in fact most astrologers themselves now use computers for this), it still can't offer the depth and complexity of interpretation that a well trained and experienced astrologer can. And it is possible, in some cases, that the computer could spew out misleading information based on differing elements in one chart. One example of this was a young man whose computer interpretation told him that the loss of his father was a strong possibility soon. Deeply troubled, he consulted a real live astrologer who helped him to understand the correct interpretation that, as they had been arguing very badly, his old relationship with his father was indeed 'dying' out, to be replaced by a new one, one with Dad very much on the scene. The best policy is to have fun reading computer printouts, but not to rely on their interpretation so seriously that it would influence any major decisions and certainly not to take dire precautions to heart.

IS THERE AN ASTROLOGER BEHIND ASTROLOGY?

It's exciting meeting and having your own session with an astrologer. Many wonder what a visit with a real astrologer will be like − for most it's a bit of an adventure into the unknown. There are important things to consider such as how to select an astrologer, what to expect from a session, what to ask, and how to evaluate it afterwards.

What image does the word astrologer conjure up? For many it is one out of old movies, the image of a slightly strange little old lady, a bead-draped hippie, or of a dark man with mysterious and penetrating eyes. While, as with all the metaphysical realms, characters of this type still do turn up, today you are just as likely to find a well-dressed professional. The quality of the session is greatly dependent on the astrologer. It's worth taking the time to investigate thoroughly, finding someone who is highly recommended. In addition to enquiring about the training and experience of an astrologer under consideration, it is wise to ask about their background and interests as well.

As suggested in the introduction, the best way to find an astrologer is to get a referral from a friend or acquaintance. This way you can ask someone who has already been there about the astrologer's style and focus. But be careful also to consider the source in evaluating their recommendation and assessment. Look at who's doing the recommending as part of the judgement in selecting whom you are going to consult. Just as you wouldn't go to a mechanic recommended by someone whose car is always breaking down, so it is unlikely someone whose life is in chaos will be the best judge of any kind of metaphysical consultant. Always evaluate your referral sources!

How To Find An Astrologer

- Referrals from friends and acquaintances.
- Local metaphysical bookseller – will often have astrologers employed there or know local ones.
- Astrological faculties and professional associations.
- Astrological magazines – have astrologers on staff and will do charts by correspondence.
- Astrologers who write columns in magazines – some accept clients by mail. If there's one you particularly like, it's worth writing to them at the magazine to see if they do readings.

If you are selecting an astrologer from one of the referral sources suggested, ask them some questions before making a decision. It is important to know how qualified they are and what orientation they take with their clients. Questions to ask about their background include:

- How many years' experience do you have as an astrologer?
- Is this your profession or do you have other work?
- In what ways did you train?
- Do you have any special interests either as a consultant or personally which enhance the way you work?

Beginners need to get experience somehow, but going to a new astrologer is like going to the local haircutting school to have a haircut. You are taking your chances. You may get the next Vidal Sassoon; you may get someone who belongs behind a lawnmower. A beginner will probably charge considerably less than a long-established professional. If you like to experiment, you don't tend to take what you hear particularly seriously, or if you go to readers often, try a beginner. But if you go rarely, and especially if you are easily influenced by what you hear, it is probably worth while to save up your money and wait to see a respected, though more costly, professional.

The fact that an astrologer makes a living from the profession is a good clue as to their quality of work. It means they have spent years building up enough clients to support themselves, and they have had a wide range of experiences with clients. But there are some very good ones who simply don't want to spend all their time at astrology, so consider this as only one aspect of the evaluation.

It is only very recently that astrological studies have been available at any orthodox educational institutions. There have been courses for study available for many years in London, and one of these, the Astrological Faculty, offers a correspondence course. But there are still fine astrologers who have studied on their own. This is why experience counts for so much in evaluation. An interesting recent development is the new generation of astrologers now appearing who also have training and are accredited psychologists.

The most important element in selection is how comfortable you feel with the consultant under consideration, because the session is likely to touch on personal matters. It also is helpful if the individual is reasonably familiar with the sort of life you lead, as they will be better able to advise in important areas. If looking into some delicate personal matters which concern a relationship or family, it may be better to see an astrologer who is also trained in counselling or psychology, and who has a family as well. If, on the other hand, your interest is focused on professional life, someone who has themselves worked in the business world and has an understanding of those needs will interpret the chart more accurately.

The matter of the astrologer's orientation and personal style of presenting information is extremely important. For example, a very independent-minded and questioning lady had a session with an astrologer whose style was to explain the client's life from conception on, through birth, and who expected her to listen and not speak. The astrologer was a well-respected consultant, and the quality of the information he gave was excellent, it just wasn't presented in a format which that particular client liked or was comfortable with.

It is worth while to consider the following questions: How independent minded am I, or do I like to have other people help plan things out? Do I need to ask questions as I go, or do I like to listen and then go away and think about what's been said? Ask the astrologer you are considering how they work, if their method is to trace the astrological history from birth or to focus on the present, if questions can be asked during the session, and if they view the information they give as destiny-orientated or viewing the options as shown in the chart.

Astrological styles fall into several categories. First of all, there is the destiny v. free will option. Destiny-orientated astrologers feel that they are interpreting fate as it is written in the planets. They tend to be event-oriented, giving dates. Free-will-orientated astrologers predict expected events, but with the attitude that the prior knowledge will enable greater benefit to be derived from any situation. They are usually much less prediction-orientated.

Then there are astrologers who focus on early life, sometimes going year by year. When they reach the present, they continue with that format, on the predictive level. Some even go back to conception, like the one mentioned earlier. Others leap right into the present, talking about what they see as concerns of the moment and near future. Some of these are destiny-orientated, some free will. One lady was told that she would never have a happy marriage. No discussion. This was obviously from a very destiny-orientated astrologer. Not at all happy with that idea, she went to another astrologer whose style focused on free will more. She was told that she did, indeed, have some serious issues to deal with in the relationship area, some lessons to learn about selecting partners, and relating with them. It would require time and a willingness to face facts but, with effort, she could learn to overcome her weaknesses, change her 'destiny' and have a well-earned happy relationship.

The extreme of destiny-orientated astrology is found in

India. There, the astrologer is consulted in almost every life situation, by parents planning the marriage of children, by businessmen when making deals, by politicians. In Indian astrology, there is very little latitude for free will and the idea is that knowing what's going to happen at least allows for preparation for the inevitable. The Indian horoscope is constructed in the same manner as a Western one, based on the birth date and time. The chart produced looks very different, not only because it is usually in Sanskrit, one of India's ancient languages, but also because of its square form. The greatest difference is the weight given in interpretation to two elements in the chart which many Western astrologers ignore. *Rahu* and *Ketu* are not planets at all, but points in space where the paths of the sun and the moon cross in orbit. In medieval times, they were more frequently used in the West, when they were referred to as the Head and Tail of the Dragon, but they are now called the north and south lunar nodes. These points in space, believed to exert such power, are often emphasised in both the Indian magazine columns (and they have more, if that is possible, than in the West) and in private consultations. Having an eighteen-year cycle of movement through the zodiac, major predictions, often dire, hinge on Rahu and Ketu's arrival in a sign. As an example of this a recent visitor to an Indian astrologer was told marriage was in the chart (no choice here!) and it would occur between the coming May and August, or failing that, in December of the following year.

Sometimes such destiny-orientated astrology serves other purposes. The majority of marriages are still arranged by the families in India, and the natal charts of prospective partners are always presented to the astrologer for approval before any commitments are made. Occasionally, when the young couple, who may only get to meet once or twice before the wedding, really don't take to each other, it is conveniently said that the astrologer did not think their charts were well suited, and the marriage plans can be abandoned without embarrassment to either of the families involved.

- LIFE READING – goes over life from childhood to present, predicts future, event-orientated. The majority are destiny-orientated.
- LIFE PSYCHOLOGICAL ANALYSIS – reviews life from childhood, especially focusing on psychological impact of parents, environments. Events are seen from this viewpoint. Dialogue between client and astrologer encouraged.
- EVENT-ORIENTATED, PREDICTIVE – focuses on present, how to make decisions, goals, what events to expect in the future, timing.
- PSYCHOLOGICAL CURRENT ANALYSIS – discusses present and upcoming events from the point of view of how one will deal with new situations and people, explores upbringing and environment as influence on current situations.

Before selecting a consultant, it is worthwhile to take the time to review and evaluate what the fundamental reason is for making an appointment and what is expected as a result. Is it that you want a new view of life, you're feeling aimless, searching for definition, wanting clarity? Then the best choice is someone who gives a life overview. If you are wrestling with a situation or decision in the present, about work or perhaps a relationship, then someone who dwells on the current situation will suit better. Planning career moves, deciding about returning to full-time study, or looking at some choices which will affect the future, will be best served by a psychologically orientated astrologer who will be better able to focus on those areas.

TAKING CARE OF BUSINESS

As usual, ask the fee and how long the session will be. While a few may ask very modest amounts, the fee will probably be comparable with that charged by any other professional consultant in the community, such as a lawyer or psychologist. For a long-established and well-known professional it may be more, less for someone newer. Sessions are usually one to two hours. Some astrologers will take much longer, as much as four or five hours, for the first consultation, so it is important to enquire about the length of time the session will last.

Ask if the session can be tape recorded. Most consultants don't mind; some actually prefer it. It is absolutely impossible to remember everything covered in a session. Notes tend to be based on what seems pertinent at the time and it is possible to ignore something that will be of great importance in the future. A tape is a clear record of the visit which can be referred to any time. Most clients find them invaluable.

YOU MAKE YOUR APPOINTMENT

When making an appointment, you will be asked to give your birth information. The birth date, place and hour of birth (or of the event) are required. As a horoscope is a map of the heavens for a place and time, this information needs to be as exact as possible. As little as four minutes can make a difference in the chart.

The policy about recording the time of birth is different from country to country, and district to district. In some countries, France in particular, and in most of the states of the USA, it is the law that birth times are recorded. In England, unfortunately, there is no such law, so unless a family member recalls the information, it can be difficult to come by. Sometimes family documents such as bibles or baby books will have the time noted in them. A little digging around is often fruitful and it is worth pressing older members of the family. They may not recall the actual time but will remember that the birth was 'near tea time', for example, or before sunrise. Oddly enough, one's own mother's memory may not be the most reliable, and any consulting astrologer can tell you that a mother often recalls the wrong time! Do the research before ringing to make the appointment. If you're asking the astrologer about another person, have their birth information ready as well.

It sometimes happens that there is no access to information about the birth time. Don't worry. Many think they can never go to an astrologer because they have no record of the time of birth. It is still possible to have your chart done. In days past when clocks were rare, techniques were developed to deal with situations of this order. The astrologer's first choice will probably be to do a solar chart, a chart done as if the birth were at dawn of the birth date. This is a remarkably accurate technique, and is used often. Though it cannot give quite as precise information about elements of timing as a chart done with a correct birth time, it reveals a surprising amount about character and major trends in life.

There is a process, called rectification, which can, after considerable calculation, determine the hour of birth. The idea behind it is that if, from a chart calculated from an accurate time of birth, forthcoming events can be predicted, then past events should be able to produce a chart with an accurate time. Using the dates of major events from the past, such as deaths of family members, major life changes, moves, marriages, and births, an astrologer gradually patches together the likely chart. Not surprisingly, this can be very time consuming and expensive. If you are interested in having this done, ask if the astrologer is trained to do this, as not all are. You should also ask what the fee will be, before getting involved in it.

WORRIED ABOUT WORDS?

When thinking about seeing an astrologer, many people are put off by the fear of being unable to understand the strange jargon used. Often in newspaper and magazine columns terms are used which would otherwise only appear in Scrabble games. In fact, there is probably more jargon in astrology than in any other area of metaphysics. While it is not necessary to become expert in the language of astrology, there are a few terms it will be helpful to know.

BASIC ASTROLOGICAL VOCABULARY

Star Sign (also Sun Sign) One of the twelve signs of the Zodiac, determined by birth date. Examples are Aries, Taurus, Gemini.

Zodiac Sign Same as star sign. Also a type of energy, a way of being.

Planet A pure force, in a horoscope is spoken of as being in a zodiac sign (e.g. Venus in the sign of Taurus). In astrology, the sun and moon are referred to as planets.

House An area of life, one of the twelve pie-shaped wedges in the chart.

Rising Sign Literally, the sign of the zodiac which was rising on the eastern horizon at the moment for which a chart has been calculated.

Aspect The relative position of two planets to each other measured geometrically.

Progression Technique of projecting planetary movements to predict future events.

Transit The positions of the planets for the day in question, usually compared to the birth horoscope for prediction.

Retrograde Apparent backward motion of a planet in the heavens, in reality an optical illusion.

Horary Technique in which chart is done for the moment a question is asked, to reveal answer.

Synastry Compares charts of individuals for relationship, or business.

These are the basic terms which might be encountered. Familiarity with them will give you enough confidence to ask questions with ease, unintimidated by the jargon. Knowledge of other astrological terms isn't really necessary, though you may find astrologers who use a lot.

Some astrologers' training did not include the translation

into common English of the special terms used in interpreting charts. Others have just got into the habit of speaking in this jargon, and clients, intimidated, never ask for clarification. It is worth remembering that the astrologer's task is to *interpret* the horoscope, otherwise you could just as well do it yourself by ordering a chart and consulting an 'astrological cookbook', the sort of reference book which has all the meanings of the positions of the planets listed and interpreted. But this is more difficult than you imagine. It would be as if a doctor handed you the results of medical tests and a medical textbook to look them up in. Since it is possible to have the chart explained in English, it is much easier to have it done that way, and if the astrologer slips into jargon, just ask for English!

YOUR FIRST TIME

Before you make the appointment, you will have decided what type of astrologer to consult and what the focus of the visit will be. Knowing what you want to find out will help direct the session.

On their first visit some people wish to focus on the natal chart and its interpretation; others prefer to sample widely from what the astrologer has to offer. It may be of interest to talk about personal relationships, family, work or career; or to ask the astrologer to evaluate how well you handle aspects of your life and if there are any attitudes which are preventing the attainment of goals. Matters of the future may be important, or perhaps knowing how to understand better and deal with another person, to help a romance along the way or to build a stronger relationship with a partner. It is possible to look at health, or to understand aspects of the psyche more clearly.

Most astrologers will probably start by investigating the natal chart in some depth. Virtually every first-time visitor is surprised by how detailed and precise the information is and how it is possible someone who has never seen you can know so much about the inner workings of your mind and your life. The astrologer will explain what the chart shows to be strengths and weaknesses of your nature. There may be qualities never consciously acknowledged which could be brought out more; weaknesses will be discussed, with the idea of understanding them in order to overcome them. Some suggestions will be given on ways to work on improving these points. Most modern astrologers consider that the whole point of the session is to give a clearer look at yourself with the idea of change.

BUT I WANT MY FORTUNE TOLD!

Long-time metaphysical explorers, who have visited many different types of readers, tell about a reversal phenomenon most experience when consulting psychics and astrologers. Clairvoyants or psychics (terms which mean the same thing) dazzle clients during the session by giving names and details, for example, of the person you were feeling guilty about not having rung, the kind of food you're going to have for dinner tomorrow night, and what colour your cat is − all things they could not possibly have known. Astrologers generally create less drama during the session because they really cannot tell by using astrology alone facts of such an exact nature.

Astrologers are far less detailed than clairvoyants in their descriptions. For example, of meeting a new romance, the astrologer will say the type of person it will be, and how they will affect your life. An approximate date will be given, with a clear 'not before' such and such a time, and ways in which you could sabotage the situation, especially if it triggers any of your own self-destruction mechanisms. But as for the colour of the eyes, alas, you'll just have to wait and see.

People who prefer the thrill of being told very exact predictions will be disappointed by this. Even the most destiny-orientated astrologers can't promise that everything they tell you will be correct.

The reversal in accuracy between the psychic and the

astrologer will come a few months later, when you listen again to the tape of the session. Some of the things the psychic said which were so exact and seemed so appealing and potentially true will not have occurred, bringing the accuracy to 50:50, while things the astrologer said, which may not have made much sense at the time, are now coming to be.

This happens because the psychic is reading from the mental energy field, the conscious thoughts, as well as those of the unconscious. The psychic describes things as they look at the moment. Later, as the future unfolds, some will evolve from the thought stage to actual events and people, depending on how much energy is put into each of the individual situations.

The astrologer, on the other hand, is looking at patterns, set up on the day of birth, pictured in the natal chart. These are far less easy to change, for some are as deeply a part of you as your eye colour. The predictions based on the chart derive from an assessment of its fundamental nature, some parts of which may not have been consciously considered before, and may therefore sound quite new the first time they are brought up. These aspects may have been submerged, with no understanding of how they influence life choices, but they are still an integral part of your nature. These are deep patterns, which do not change without conscious effort. The predictions based on these patterns will probably be very accurate.

It is from recognition of these deep patterns that some astrologers derive their fatalistic way of giving information in a session. From time to time, astrologers will try to dazzle their clients with detail like a psychic, or by claiming never to be wrong. One lady encountered an astrologer who was very much of the destiny persuasion. The woman was planning a very long trip abroad, and was told by the astrologer that she would have to have emergency surgery while she was away. A nervous traveller on the best days, and understandably upset by this revelation, she questioned the astrologer as to how she could avoid it, and if she could take preventative measures? She had a history of medical difficulties, so this really triggered her fears. But she couldn't see how anything could be so drastic as to warrant surgery! The astrologer told her client that she was never wrong, and guaranteed she would give the client her money back if she did not end up needing surgery! The client was so overwhelmed by worry she did not take the trip – and stayed home in perfect health.

ASTROLOGICAL TOUR – DIFFERENT KINDS OF ASTROLOGY

In most people's minds astrology is so intimately associated with the idea of portraying the individual characteristics shown in the natal chart that it doesn't even occur to them that astrology can be used in other ways. But there are lots of other techniques which can be employed.

ASTROLOGICAL TECHNIQUES

These elaborate the information presented in the birth or natal chart.

Progressed charts and transits Both are predictive methods, derived from the natal chart, which focus on events in life, inner changes and their timing.

Relationship Synastry uses techniques of comparing two individuals' natal charts, and also making one chart from the two by creating a literal composite of the two charts involved. Used in business and in personal counselling.

Infant and child An aid to child rearing, used for a better understanding of the child's fundamental nature and needs, the most appropriate types of education. It compares the child's chart with those of the parents.

Psychological Used by astrologically trained psychologists to evaluate and treat clients.

Medical Diagnosis Treatment of illness, studying the
body's needs.
Nutritional Studies body type to select diet to best suit
the individual.
Career Counselling based on interests and abilities seen
in chart, in youth for training, in adulthood for
timing of possible career changes.

And there is a range of astrological services which use
the position of the planets to assess trends, and to predict
events in the world:
Business Used to time changes in business, plan cor-
porate strategy, assess prospective employees.
Financial Astrological specialists advise on trends in
financial markets.
Political Predicts the outcome of elections, looking at
the charts of politicians and rulers, and of countries
to predict economic and social changes.
Sports Analyses players and teams, and even horses(!)
in order to pick winners.
Weather One of astrology's most ancient applications,
predicts weather changes, storms, droughts.
Geological Predicts earthquakes.

BOOKS AND COURSES

Before studying astrology in more depth, you need to
become familiar first with the types of books available.
There are three distinct classes and the divisions between
them can be based on the level of knowledge of the reader.
The first group, for those with general interest, but little
previous technical knowledge, maintains a general focus,
usually based around the twelve star signs. The second
group is for those who wish to learn more about the subject
and comprises, in essence, primers, teaching the symbols

employed in astrology and their meaning. It is possible to gain a foundation from these books, and some of them are excellent. The third type is designed for those 'fluent' in astrology, that is those who know the basic meaning of the symbols for the signs, planets and can read a chart. The gap between the second and the third type is very large, and it is for this reason that many begin to study astrology in classes; it is simply not a subject which can be easily learned from books.

Popular books remain the largest classification in terms of titles and of sales, each year bringing more to the book-sellers' shelves. The beginning of the explosion of the popular type of astrology book began in the early 70s when Linda Goodman wrote a book about the twelve signs. It was the start of an avalanche, continuing to this day, of books which describe the characteristics of the signs of the zodiac. A consulting astrologer herself, she had worked with and come to understand the astrological types very well indeed. The book, *Sun Signs*, has become a classic, and adorns the bookshelves of anyone with even a passing interest in astrology. It could almost be viewed as the foundation upon which has been built a vast empire of sun sign astrology literature.

Since then, there have been hundreds of other titles, which have taken the concept as far as the star sign theme could possibly go! In addition to shelves full of star sign character analysis books, there have been star sign sex books, cookbooks, books on how each star sign should dress, and star-sign nutrition. There are actresses who have become 'expert' astrologers who write books on star sign beauty. There is even a star sign pet book. This industry has produced some amusing books, and made a lot of money for the authors, but it is questionable how far the star sign theme can go and keep any accuracy, value and integrity.

Whatever the level of knowledge, the overwhelming choice can make looking for a book a dizzying experience. Rather than be left standing stunned in a big store, unable to make a selection and with no hope of a helpful sales assistant, it is worth calling in at a specialist booksellers, or even ringing a centre or school for a recommendation beforehand. Once you are on to the right sort of book, it becomes easier because the better books usually have bibliographies which will list other books and authors worth a look.

STUDIES

There are two approaches which can be taken to the study of astrology. One is the more casual approach, reading books of interest, perhaps attending the odd class or lecture. Many who start out this way become very knowledgeable and are able to interpret charts and sometimes even calculate them. The drawback to this manner of study is that studying done according to natural interest rather than following a programme often leaves gaps in the knowledge.

The second approach is to follow a formal plan of study. Large centres specialising in metaphysical studies sometimes offer courses. Occasionally astrologers who do private consulting teach as well. Perhaps the best bet, especially if you are considering astrology as a career, is to take one of the correspondence courses offered through astrological faculties. Carefully organised to cover topics ranging from history, astronomy, mathematics, and even psychology, as well as giving a fine grounding in the range of astrological techniques, completion of a course of this sort is likely to supply the student with both knowledge and confidence.

YOUR FUTURE WITH ASTROLOGY

For the informed, astrology is more than just the star signs. It embraces all the energies of our planet and the rhythms in which they flow. And once the area becomes a familiar one, the range of options for exploration is vast and intriguing.

Casual reading of star sign columns and popular books can be enhanced by awareness of how best to use the information they offer. The occasional casual visit to an astrologer is enhanced by some knowledge of the process and of what can be asked and expected. For those who consult an astrologer on a more serious basis, having a sense of the character and depth of information available will make the visit more profitable.

Pursuits of those who choose to study further can range from learning about the energy types portrayed in star sign astrology, or the deeper investigation into the individual nature, as with natal astrology. It offers ways to examine career options, improve self-understanding, and relationships. There is a choice of approaches, either using a destiny orientation or taking a more psychological direction. If health and fitness is a focus, astrology and the body would be an area to explore. Interested in finance? Astrologers' studies of the market cycles over the years will be a foundation for research.

For those who want to structure their learning formal study may be ideal, and for some there's the possibility of becoming a consultant and using astrology for others' benefit.

The realm is yours to explore.

7

Cartomancy – the Future from Cards

On the screen in the cinema, an old gypsy slowly lays out cards covered with strange and mysterious symbols before a wide-eyed young lady. When a particularly menacing looking card appears, the old woman becomes grave, and, quickly gathering up the cards, says 'Go away! I can tell you nothing today.'

Are you one of those afraid this will happen if you consult a card reader? As melodramatic as the scenario seems, it is not unusual for the cards to evoke a sense of dread and many, even those familiar with other areas of metaphysics, experience this. For these, the cards have dark and occult associations and the fear persists of what might be unveiled by them, resulting in the same uncertain terror.

Of all the areas of the sixth sense, the cards most seem to arouse such fears. Cartomancy is the term meaning the use of cards to reveal the nature of situations and their probable outcome. No matter what sort of cards are used, either an ancient, picturesque Tarot deck or ordinary playing cards, cartomancy is an ancient method for looking into the future. Despite their indelible association with the occult, cards can present an alarmingly accurate picture of a situation and its likely outcome. This has been enough to earn them quite a mystique, not to mention a spooky aura. But do they deserve it?

We often say, 'It's all in the cards,' meaning an unchangeable situation or one out of our power. The way this phrase
is used reflects the belief that the cards somehow have a
power to reveal and influence fate. Certainly, of all the
devices used for looking into the future, it is easiest to
endow the cards themselves with the power of creating the
future because they show it so picturesquely. And for some,
the leap to believing that the fall of the cards themselves
somehow shapes the future is not a great one. Of course,
the cards don't really shape the future. But they do portray
it. The cards mirror what is unfolding at the moment
they are dealt.

The mechanism behind this utilises the energy field
which surrounds each of us. As its contents are a direct
result of our thoughts and desires, moods and attitudes,
both those conscious and unconscious, a device for reading it will reveal its secrets. (For more about this, see
Chapter 8 on clairvoyants and psychics.) An example of
this would be a friend who senses your mood before you
even say a word, by reading the energies you are sending
out. While a friend may be able to sense a mood, the
cards are designed to mirror the energies more precisely.
As they are shuffled for a reading, and are laid out, their
evocative symbols present the energy in picture form.
Many see the cards as having fallen 'by chance' rather
than as a reflection of the state of mind of the enquirer.
Taking that point of view, it is but an easy step to blame
the cards entirely for one's fate. And many would be
delighted to do so.

A difficult concept for many to grasp, the fact is that
whatever kind of cards are being read, they are only a
mirror of the future *as it stands in the present*. They are an
exact reflection of the state of things at the moment of the
session and especially of any particular situation being
asked about. Their purpose is to reveal the nature of that
situation. The cards do not reveal a 'fated' destiny. It is

true that if from the time of the reading absolutely nothing is changed, no attitudes altered or matters dealt with, then events will go almost exactly as they have been pictured in the cards. If, however, shifts are made, or immediate action taken, then a reading done as little as five minutes after the initial one would come out with a substantially different prediction. Destiny is not changed by changing the way the cards fall; when destiny is altered the cards will reflect that change.

In order to take best advantage of any card reading session, it is helpful to be aware of this. Experience proves this point, and improves the understanding of the process of a reading. Every card reader has at least once been badgered by a client into laying out the cards a second time because the client didn't like what the cards had to say the first. After the client goes through the whole process of thoroughly shuffling and dealing the cards again, amazingly, very nearly all of the original cards will appear a second time.

THE GYPSIES' BIBLE?

Card readings are done with two major types of cards: Tarot cards and the familiar playing cards. The picturesque Tarot cards are what you probably imagined in the movie scene mentioned above. Rich with symbols, forms and colours, Tarot cards are particularly associated with gypsies, who have used the cards since their earliest history. There is a tradition that the Tarot cards were the gypsies' bible. The images of their philosophy and teachings were pictured on the cards. It is possible that the original gypsy tribes came to Europe from India, via Egypt (where they picked up their name), bringing the Tarot with them.

The Tarot deck is organised in a similar way to today's playing cards. It has four suits, corresponding to those in playing cards, though called by different names. Its cards are numbered from ace to ten, and the court cards are the same, though the Tarot court has an extra member, the page, who has been lost in modern playing cards. What most differentiates the Tarot from today's deck is the Tarot's extra twenty-two cards. These have almost totally disappeared from modern playing cards; the only remnant is the Joker, derived from the Fool card in the Tarot.

The additional twenty-two cards are known as the Major Arcana. The word arcana means secret or hidden; these cards are the part of the gypsy 'bible' in which information reserved for the initiated is given in symbols. It is likely that these cards were not originally intended for use in telling fortunes. Though the entire Tarot deck has an undeniable mystique, the highly symbolic cards of the Major Arcana are an invitation to deeper reflection. The images of the cards are haunting and evocative even to the untutored eye, some with obvious meanings, others less clear, but all promising secret wisdom revealed to those who are willing to study to lift the veil.

There are many versions of Tarot card decks. While they are all composed of the same suits and the same cards in the Major Arcana, the design and the symbols used vary widely. While the oldest deck existing dates from 1392 and was made for the French King Charles VI, the one most commonly seen today, the Marseilles Tarot, was recorded in the writings of Court [sic] de Gebelin in eighteenth-century France. Old even when he wrote of it, it is colourful and engaging with evocative symbols. There is an obvious resemblance between its court cards and those of today's ordinary playing cards, which are, indeed, descended from this version of the Tarot.

A more recent version often seen today is called the Waite or the Rider deck. Dating from the first decade of this century, they were designed by Edward Arthur Waite, an English scholar of the occult, and drawn by Pamela Colman Smith. The deck incorporates symbols used in the Marseilles Tarot with those from numerous other mystical traditions such as the Egyptian and Hebrew and

Christian. Each card in the Waite deck has a wealth of symbolism.

Though there is no single book which provides a comprehensive guide to the Tarot, Waite himself wrote one designed to accompany his deck. Even that book really only points out what the symbols are on each of the cards, and suggests what they mean in a reading. The range of possible interpretations for each card is very wide, and the Tarot demands personal study and reflection in order to even begin to gain an understanding of it. There is no way to become an instant expert on the Tarot.

Growing interest in the Tarot has resulted in a variety of new decks designed over the past twenty years. Well over one hundred different ones are available, ranging from Aquarian Age decks to feminist decks. They are available for comparison at stores stocking metaphysical books and supplies. With the variety of images portrayed in the cards, and the amount of interpretation required on the part of the reader, it is helpful to use a deck with sympathetic images which are comfortable to relate to.

FOOLS AND DEVILS

The cards of the Major Arcana reflect the full range of life situations, aspirations and depths. In the cards a hierarchy of government is present: the Emperor card and the Empress, the Pope, often called the Heirophant, and the agents of Justice and the Last Judgement. So are life's conditions, the Lovers, Strength, Temperance; and the symbols for them, the Sun, the Moon, and the Star. The rulers of the occult world are there as well: the Magician and the High Priestess, and the card made famous in the Beatles' song, the Fool. All these cards appear, though with slightly different names, in every version of the Tarot deck.

The symbols on the cards have a wide variety of interpretations. Even the seemingly most obvious ones have many levels of meaning. For example, the Death card of the Rider deck has a skeleton in armour on horseback. Though the meaning may seem pretty obvious, a closer look reveals other options: the horse is white, not normally the colour of death, and the knight bears a banner with the rosy cross, an ancient symbol of rebirth. In the card, the king falls before the skeletal knight, and a bishop receives him; in the background the sun is rising, symbol of the new day dawning. The card is a card of passing, it is true, but of a situation which is being reborn (the rising sun) into a new form.

The images in each of the cards of the Major Arcana are as complex. Though each card merits study on its own, for those interested in learning more of the cards, one of the best methods is by spreading them out and comparing them with each other. Some are obviously designed to be viewed as pairs. The Emperor and the Empress; the Magician and the High Priestess; and, surprisingly, the Lovers and the Devil. Each card shows a man and a woman standing in front of a being of mythic proportion. In the Lovers, a prettily coloured card, the pair are before an Angel, whose arms are raised over them in benediction. But in the background, behind the woman, is the Tree of Life with the waiting serpent entwined in its branches. Is Paradise not to last? Apparently not, because in the Devil card the same couple appears, considerably less jolly looking, as they stand against a black background underneath a very disagreeable Devil. The couple each have a chain around their neck attached to the Devil's platform. This chain is actually loose enough to remove, had each the wit to do so. Is there escape from this grim fate? Apparently, if only they would notice the possibility.

In each card, and in its relationship with the others, lies the potential to reveal all of life's conditions and situations – a complex study. This is why the reading of Tarot cards is no casual matter. While it is possible to buy a deck of cards and a book and play at doing readings for friends, this will only be scratching the surface of the meaning

and could lead to misinterpretation of some of the cards.
After all, who would think a card with a Fool on it would
be one of the best cards?

SYMBOLS IN TAROT CARDS

The Suits	Each represents an area of endeavour, type of temperament and of colouring. (Note, in a reading, the temperament may override the colouring in deciding the appropriate suit.)
Wands (now Clubs)	Will and power, work on the land and with commerce and goods; enterprising, fertile, earthy, energetic, warm; fair haired and light eye colour.
Cups (now Hearts)	Knowledge and continuation, work at the professions, and with ideas; help others, are loving, sensitive, generous; medium brown hair and hazel eyes.
Swords (now Spades)	Activity, work at big business, military; are decisive, strong, unemotional, intense; deep brown hair and eyes.
Pentacles or **Dinars** (now Diamonds)	Money, industry, work in a creative and imaginative way whether in trade or professions; are powerful, charismatic, brooding; have intense colouring be it darkest dark or very fair.

THE SYMBOLS ON THE CARDS

Roses

Life eternal, from the Rosy Cross, the symbol of the Medieval Mystical Society.

Lilies

Life after death, the eternal soul, purity.

Note: the above two are combined as a motif in many of the cards. In that case the implication is of the many levels of reality.

Drops (Yods, 'God's Dew')

Drops of light, and of God's wisdom, skill.

Sun

Hope, possibilities, creative energy overcoming all obstacles.

Moon

Reflected light, the subconscious, situations not fully seen or understood.

Hand from Cloud

Divine intervention or opportunity.

Water

The flow of life itself, emotions.

Leaves

Growth, vitality.

Crescent and Butterfly

The soul.

Crown

Mastery in the world.

Figure 8 Sideways

Infinity, a view beyond the present, a larger purpose.

INTERPRETATION, NOT READING

Though cards are 'read', they are not read as a book would be; they are interpreted. Each individual card has a wealth of symbols with many options for interpretation, and the meanings change when the cards appear next to other cards. A good 'reader' must develop the skill of blending the meanings together.

As with many of the areas of metaphysical study, the experience of the person who is reading will make a great difference to its quality. Age is not necessarily a factor, though, as some very young readers grew up in families where Granny got out a pack of cards after Sunday lunch, and became familiar with the cards as children. In fact, of all the metaphysical fields, this is one where simple experience and exposure bring the greatest knowledge. Card-reading techniques may be taught in a class, but are best learned by experience.

It is still possible for even the most experienced reader to have unclear patches, though. For example, having gone for a general reading, a woman was told by the reader that the cards showed she would have a baby quite soon. Having no boyfriend, much less a husband, it seemed a strongly unlikely prospect at the time. She queried this and was assured by the reader that she was quite sure the prediction would be correct. Shrugging her shoulders and dismissing it, the woman forgot the matter until she encountered another woman who had also had a reading from the same reader. The woman had also been told that she would be having a baby, as had some of her friends as well. It seemed that the reader was considering having a child herself and was seeing babies everywhere!

All readers will have areas where their capacity to detach themselves from their own world is limited. While a true professional will reduce the distortion to a minimum, the wise client will quickly question anything that seems inappropriate or troubling. While slightly uncomfortable facts or truths could well appear in a good reading, if anything really troubling is said, the best policy is speak up at once. The problem may only be a matter of misunderstanding. Not only will questioning lead to clarification; it may actually help the reader be more specific as well.

PLAYING CARDS

Descendants from the mysterious Tarot deck, today's 'ordinary' playing cards have the same heritage, and in the right hands the same power to tell fortunes. While it is still possible to lose when gambling with these, a knowledgeable reader can also use the same cards to tell the future. Because playing cards lack the twenty-two Major Arcana which give the Tarot their mystical impact, a reading from playing cards will probably have a more mundane focus. It will deal more with day-to-day matters, practical affairs, where the Tarot would probe into deeper motivations as well.

When used in fortune telling the number of cards is usually reduced from the normal fifty-two to thirty-two, using only those from seven or higher. Unlike Tarot cards, with their wide range of possible interpretations, each card has a very precise meaning; but as with Tarot cards, each suit is associated with a fundamental temperament, aspect of life and colouring. Equally all cards of a particular number have a meaning, for example, all aces are messages, opportunities, possibilities; sevens are uncertain and mean change.

When you use playing cards it is especially easy to become fatalistic about the outcome. For example, a reading composed mostly of spades, often a troublesome suit, could lead you to blame them for difficulties; but it is better to remember that these cards only mirror the state of the moment. If the cards are viewed as a recap of the situation, then the reading can be seen to give information which can be used in remedying it. It is also to be remembered that a wonderful reading is not a signal to lie back, relax and stop making an effort.

THE LADY WHO WAS REFUSED A READING

The phenomenon of cards changing with the mood and attitude of the client is familiar to readers. So much so that some will not do a reading when a client is in a very negative frame of mind. An example of this occurred when a woman in distress and greatly concerned over a situation went to see her reader. The reader told her she preferred not to lay out the cards just then as the client's state of mind was so negative she felt it would darkly colour the reading. She suggested that the client wait two days before coming back, and she would then lay out the cards. When the woman called in again, she had a reading which gave her a useful view of the situation.

WHEN YOU GO

Card readings can range in length from a few minutes to several hours. They can range in intensity from a quick glimpse at one's luck for betting at the races to peering into past lives via the Tarot cards. Whichever the type of reading, certain elements of the process, which is almost like a ritual, are the same.

Most readers discuss the general reason for the reading before it starts. Give them an idea of your concerns; enquire when you may ask questions. Some readers do prefer to get the first view of the situation from the cards themselves, uninfluenced by questions. Others prefer to know at the outset what to focus on.

Every reading begins with shuffling the cards. Cards, especially Tarot cards, are not usually handled by anyone but the reader, and are kept out of sight, often wrapped in a silk scarf, when not in use. During the shuffling the cards are filled with the client's energy. Some readers shuffle a specific number of times, but it is more usual to continue until 'the cards feel full of your energy'. Next the cards will be cut, probably with the left hand.

The reader will then gather up the cards and may select a 'significator', the card representing the client in the reading. Based on the traditional attributes for colouring and temperament of the cards, this will be removed from the deck and treated as the base card for the reading.

There are countless patterns in which the cards can be laid out. Most readers have their favourites. It is rare for every card to be used in a reading, the usual number being ten to twelve. The type of reading and the sort of information needed are factors in the choice of layout as well.

Some clients wonder just how much information can be obtained about others in their life from a card reading. Partners, lovers, friends, colleagues, are all important and it is natural to want to know about them and their influence. Most readings will show quite a lot about others, especially if they are relevant to the client's life. As it is the client's vibration which goes into the cards, the stronger the client's connections with a person or a situation, the more likely they are to appear in a reading. The circumstances of a partner's work would be likely to come up, as this would be of importance in the client's life, but a friend's relationship would not be as likely to appear unless it had some impact on the client's life. Occasionally, however, things will show in a reading which appear to be totally unrelated. But as the future unfolds, the reason for the connection becomes apparent.

Even the most experienced reader will predict things which do not come to pass. In your card reading it is your actions and reactions for the time of the reading which are revealed. Therefore, while a reading may suggest that a particular event will occur, it may well not happen in the way you expect if it involves others, as they could well alter their behaviour. On the other hand, readings will sometimes suggest developments which seem quite unlikely at the time, which only come to pass as the result of others changing their plans.

WHAT YOU CAN – AND CAN'T – FIND OUT IN A CARD READING

When going for a reading, most people have something they are especially keen to know but feel silly asking. Some are afraid that if they pluck up the courage to ask, the reader will say it isn't possible to see that from the cards. Experience will show what can be learned from a reading and what can't. Below are a sample of the most frequently asked questions that can be answered by cards, and some that can't as well.

Questions That Can Be Answered By Using Cards

- Is this the best choice of partner/job/home?
- How can I understand my partner better?
- What can I do to be more successful at work?
- What can I do to be happier/to make my partner happier?
- How can I help my children?

Questions That Cannot Be Answered By Using Cards

- Will I be happy?
- Will I be successful?
- Will he/she love me?
- Will I be healthy?
- Will my children do well at school?

As becomes apparent from this list, a question which completely hands the power in the situation over to the cards cannot possibly be answered properly. A reading may show you having everything you ever dreamed of. It may foretell a wonderful partner and home, pleasant work and an enjoyable life, perfect children. But since pleasure can't be derived solely from a situation, then 'happiness' will not come in the sense asked.

It is tempting to demand that the cards say what we want to hear, that we can expect events which will make us happy. Unfortunately, there are plenty of readers who will, for the fee for a session, regularly promise the moon. Never mind that the moon never quite appears as promised – all that is forgotten by the next time you go for another fix of an optimistic future.

THE BEST THE CARDS HAVE TO OFFER

When going for a reading, most people hope to hear of an optimistic future. But the best reading may sometimes be the worst. Instead of hearing that everything will be rosy, there may be some facts that need to be faced, actions taken, and serious matters to be dealt with. Yet this can be the best sort of reading, as it can target problem areas before they grow larger.

At its best, a card reading slices through life, giving a picture for the moment it is done. It will reveal all the flaws, as well as the high points, and a good reader will also give a view of what actually needs to be dealt with *now* in order to get things in order. The cards can help clarify and organise matters needing to be dealt with.

The cards are best used as a mirror. When things are going well, it will be wonderful to have them validate this. But when things are not as wonderful, the cards will show exactly what's wrong and where the repair work needs to begin. The worst of situations can be repaired; all that is required is commitment, a focused goal and energy.

The cards can guide and inform. They will never change your destiny, but you can do that. Isn't it nice to know that the cards will then reflect your achievements?

8

Clairvoyants and Psychics

Is there anything more seductive than the thought of knowing the future? The stuff of myths and fairy tales, those who have what is variously called 'the Vision' or 'the Sight', have been held in awe by society. Often this is mixed with suspicion, usually inspired by intimidation and ignorance. But many of these people are treated with respect, due to an understanding of the methods used by those who penetrate the future and report back on what they see.

Clairvoyants and psychics form what is perhaps the most public aspect of the realm of the sixth sense. Its proponents present themselves in a variety of styles, ranging from the familiar and easily caricatured clairvoyants who display their skills in a form which is virtually entertainment in theatres, to the quietly serious psychics who, in addition to private clients, give their time to scientific research in an effort to discover how the mechanism of their gift functions. Between these two lies a broad spectrum of individuals each of whom has unique gifts to offer.

Knowing that clairvoyants rely on nothing but their 'vision', many people find it difficult not to be intimidated by them and their world. As with all the kingdoms of the sixth sense, knowledge helps to relieve these anxieties. Learning more about those who move with ease from the limitations of the present prepares you for a visit to that exciting realm which crosses the barriers of time and place.

WHAT IS CLAIRVOYANCE?

The word clairvoyant means to 'see clearly', but even those who have consulted one remain puzzled as to how they do see. Using no charts such as an astrologer would use, nor even taking a peek at the palm, clairvoyants stun visitors by revealing facts they could have no logical way of knowing. More worryingly, they seem to be able to make predictions which are correct often enough to alarm those who are attached to more familiar ways of acquiring information.

A psychic or clairvoyant, terms which can be used interchangeably, employs a vision which extends beyond the limits of the normal five senses that the rest of us use. Quite literally the sixth sense, this vision reaches into other times, both past and future, other places and even into other minds. While all psychics have this extended capacity to see, amongst them there is a surprising variety of ways they perceive and hear information. Extra-sensory perception, usually happily shortened to ESP, is the term most often used to describe all the types of clairvoyant vision.

VOCABULARY

ESP (extra-sensory perception) The 'sixth sense', capacity to receive information other than through the five physical senses.

PSI The term for ESP currently used in scientific studies.

Psychic An individual skilled at receiving information from the world beyond the normal five senses.

Oracle, prophet A psychic, usually one who makes public proclamations and predicts events which will affect large numbers of people.

Clairvoyance Literally, clear-seeing. The ability to see beyond the physical plane. The term has come to be used to mean psychic.

Clairaudience The ability to hear sounds which do not originate from the physical plane. May hear the voices of spirits, or of events from a time past or future.

Psychometry The ability to read information psychically from an object or a place.

Intuition Extended awareness beyond the normal five senses, coming in unexpected flashes; usually refers to individuals who are untrained as psychics.

The Other Side Plane of existence beyond the physical in which reside all spirit entities.

Spirit Non-physical being who dwells on the other side, may once have been human or not.

Ghost Spirit of a deceased human.

Poltergeist Literally 'noisy ghost'. Not truly a spirit, but the manifestation of psychic energy into sounds and physical plane events such as objects flying through the air.

Spiritualism Belief that life continues after death in spirit form, and those spirits return to speak through others.

Medium Individual through whom spirit speaks.

Spirit guide Entity who appears regularly to a medium as a connection with the spirit world or the 'other side'.

Seance Session, the goal of which is to reach spirit world through a medium.

Channel Contemporary term for medium, usually applied to individual through whom a long-dead entity speaks.

Trance Unconscious state in which some mediums and channels allow other entities to speak through them.

Automatic writing Writing apparently guided by force outside the writer, assumed to be a spirit.

Ouija board Device for communicating with the spirit world using a large board with letters and numbers and a small platform which is guided by the spirits to spell out answers to questions.

Scrying Use by a psychic of reflector such as mirror, crystal ball, or water as an instrument to receive visions.

ARE YOU AN INTUITIVE?

There are many who, while they would never consider themselves to be clairvoyant, have had personal encounters with ESP. Some are reluctant to admit it at first, but the number who report such experiences is surprisingly large, as an informal poll of most people's circle of friends will prove. Two types of events are most common. The first is a sense, or intuition, that something is going to happen, most often to a family member or a friend. The second type is connected with seeing a spirit, either in a haunted place, or very often a 'visit' when a death of someone close is occurring. Intuitions may be about happy events, such as an image of a wedding, baby, or new home, though the ones concerning tragic situations such as an unexpected accident, or a death, seem to be more memorable. Information can come in a dream, or in a waking vision and may not even be thought of as precognitive until remembered when the event actually occurs. Spirit sightings are usually a surprise to those who have them, as few expect a visit of this type.

For most who receive them, psychic impressions are a rare, rather alarming and not necessarily welcome phenomenon. Not thinking of themselves as having any intuitive capacity, the recipients often feel in some way responsible, especially when a distressing image becomes reality. This is emphatically not true, as in all cases of psychic vision the viewer is only a channel for the vision, but remembering this is difficult for those unaccustomed to seeing in this way.

A few receive 'messages' frequently; those who get them often are called natural intuitives or sensitives, individuals gifted with psychic powers. Even those who have had these abilities since childhood don't always know how to interpret what they see and must wait for the 'sight' to come when it pleases. When trained, the sensitive learns how to call on it at will, accurately interpret the images seen and explain them to others. Though we all have some potential for ESP, and some may have it to a notable degree, if it is not developed by training, it remains an unreliable resource.

By way of illustrating this, it could be said that, though everyone has a speaking voice, and some may even be able to sing as well, very few voices have the potential to sing as a great opera singer would, and even then that natural gift needs to be trained in order for the artist to be able to use the voice skilfully and to rely on it performance after performance.

In exactly the same way, the potential for psychic powers, though present, must be developed in order to be reliable, to be called on at will and to be able to look clearly into the realm of the sixth sense. While the capacity is a gift, as is the voice of an opera singer, not everyone who has the vocal raw material becomes a great musical artist; nor does everyone who has psychic potential develop their abilities into a refined resource.

DEVELOPING POWERS

The natural intuitive must study to develop those talents into a reliable skill. Metaphysical centres often offer this sort of class as part of their curriculum, and consulting psychics sometimes teach classes themselves, through centres or privately. While psychic powers can be learned about in a book, psychic skills cannot be developed from a book any more than a book can teach you how to ride a bicycle. This kind of training requires experience and the guidance of a teacher. The student of psychic studies will learn about the realm they are penetrating, its structure, nature and laws. They will learn how to control their powers, how to protect themselves when probing both the unseen realms and the psyches of others. Techniques will be given for clarifying visions and for developing the grounded accuracy which differentiates a trained psychic from the amateur. The teacher will observe the student and comment on 'blind spots', areas of intuition needing to be developed. Under the teacher's guidance, the student will learn to interpret images seen and translate them in a way understandable to the client. Psychic powers are best developed not only by studying the realm, but by observing a teacher's skill and experience at calling on those powers and use of them.

And in the world of extra-sensory perception, what exactly are the powers which are developed? The answer is Psi. Psi is letter from the Greek alphabet, and is used in science to mean an unknown quantity. The Psi power is the ability to receive information which comes not from any one of the five physical senses, but from the plane beyond. A pronounced ability to see reliably into the realms of the sixth sense seems to be a gift from birth. It also seems to run in families. This may be hereditary but it is possible the environment may strongly influence this capacity as well. Recent studies have shown those who believe in psychic powers normally have better results in tests done in scientific settings than those who do not believe in them at all, suggesting that belief in the ability contributes greatly to its function. Familiarity with the realm may also develop psychic gifts further.

WHAT PSYCHICS SEE WHEN THEY LOOK

The way that information appears to psychics is almost as varied as the number of individuals with Psi powers. In this era of specialisation, the realm of the sixth sense is up to date and has specific terms for each of its skills. While all of the powers to see beyond the normal senses could be termed 'psychic', each way of viewing has its own name.

Psychics 'sense' more than see, receiving an impression or an image, sometimes even feeling through the senses of the person for whom they are reading. The true clairvoyants, 'clear-*seers*', perceive visually people, places of the past, present and future. They see auras, the ever-changing colours of the energy field which surround each of us all the time. And they see spirits – sometimes their own guides who give them information and sometimes beings from the client's life as well who appear with advice and greetings. Others' skills focus on the ability to hear voices, messages from their guides, from those who have died recently, from beings on other planes; these people are clairaudients, 'clear-*hearers*'. Those who can *communicate* with others, 'mind-readers', are telepathic. Mediums use a form of clair-audience, hearing the voices of ghosts and of recently departed relatives, while those who bring forth information from other entities through their own bodies, often while in a trance, are called channels. The capacity to read information psychically from objects is called psychometry.

Psychics tend to specialise, though the techniques they use will often overlap. Do not assume, for example, that simply because someone is psychic they will be able to contact a recently departed relative.

ANIMALS, ORACLES AND SCRYERS

In the ancient world psychics were part of the everyday landscape. Without the intrusion of science, the world was full of magic and prediction. While some of the ancient arts which have been handed down from this time have had lasting value, such as astrology and many forms of folk medicine, some seem slightly more questionable viewed in today's light. One such speciality of interpretation was haruspication, reading animal entrails for omens and auguries. In response to an enquiry, the priest would ritually cut open an animal, observe if the organs were sound, properly placed and free of disease. If they were unafflicted, the interpretation was positive for the question at hand.

Then there were the oracles, a sort of clairvoyant for the ruling classes. In pre-Christian times temple priests, but more usually priestesses, acted as oracles. Their job was to keep the rulers informed about those around them, and important matters like palace plots, and the potential success of battles. The famous Oracle at Delphi, in ancient Greece, was the source of many legends as the result of her predictions. The Oracle consisted of many priestesses (all called Pythia); she answered questions while sitting above a chasm in the earth which belched sulphurous fumes; it must have created a certain atmosphere (and may have made her 'high', enabling her to be more psychic). As the Oracle, she gave answers which ranged from the precise to the ironic. A witty example of this is when Croesus, perhaps better known for his wealth than for his ability at battle, asked if his attack against the Persians would be successful. He was told by the Oracle that 'he would destroy a great empire'. She neglected to mention it would be his own that would fall.

The most famous predictive prophet was Nostradamus. In spite of the fact that he made his predictions four hundred years ago, some are still coming to pass even today. The sixteenth-century Frenchman, known as much in his time as a physician and a scholar as for his psychic feats, used the technique of *scrying* to make his predictions. Suspending a bowl of water on a tripod, he would stare into it until, in a trance, he envisioned events in the future. He wrote down what he saw in *The Centuries*, each consisting of one hundred four-line predictions. Poetic and symbolic, they are not all clear in their meaning, even for those conversant in the medieval French in which they were written. There have, nevertheless, been quite a few precise and correct predictions, enough to establish him as an oracle of impressive accuracy. History has shown that he made numerous correct predictions about the rise and fall of monarchs and of regimes. An early illustration of this was only four years after the publication of *The Centuries*; the unfortunate king of France, Henri II, was the subject of a quatrain. Nostradamus foretold his demise from wounds to his eye made in spite of his golden helmet. The king died from injuries as the result of a broken lance which pierced his visor when jousting.

> The young lion will overcome the old one
> On the field of battle in a single combat:
> He will put out his eyes in a cage of gold:
> Two wounds, and then to die a cruel death.*

From today's vantage point, over four hundred years later, many of Nostradamus's predictions have not come true, or are too vague to tell. Yet events still occur which do seem to be as described in the verses. The coming of Khomeni to Iran, overthrowing the Shah, the death of the Kennedy brothers in America, the rapid increase of pollution as a worldwide issue, are all described. His greatest accuracy has seemed to be in matters political, for though he did correctly predict the Great London Fire of 1666, he has not seemed to be so accurate about geological changes.

In 1980 a movie was made in America about Nostradamus's predictions. In it were dramatised many of his historically correct predictions. Also dramatised in the movie was a major earthquake, yet to occur, the moviemakers having interpreted the verses as predicting it for

* From *The Prophecies of Nostradamus*, translated and edited by Erika Cheetham, Corgi Books, 1975.

May of 1988 in Los Angeles. Because of Nostradamus's accuracy over the centuries and the fact that Los Angeles does have serious earthquakes from time to time, as May of 1988 rolled around the prediction in the movie was much publicised on radio and television. For a few weeks, Los Angeles was grasped in earthquake mania, the residents preparing for the worst. Yet there was no earthquake. Whether it was the prophet himself or the movie-makers who were wrong, nothing happened and Los Angeles remained unmoved by Nostradamus's predictions.

PAST PERFECT

The greatest problem with psychic prediction is that because it focuses on the future, it takes some time to know which prediction will turn out to be the one which is accurate. After all, we're still waiting to see if some of the things Nostradamus said four hundred years ago are correct.

Visitors to a psychic or a clairvoyant have the same problem. They have to evaluate how likely what has been predicted is to happen.

Psychics hear voices, see symbols or images which must be interpreted. They may have as their 'guide' a long-dead Chinese scholar who has little experience with the modern world. Sometimes psychics themselves live in a very sheltered world and may not have the reference points to make appropriate predictions for the client. A psychic from a culture other than the client's will not be able to be accurate, or may find that their cultural values vary, so that what the psychic perceives as worrying may be absolutely fine for the client. For example, an English career woman consulted a well-known and respected Indian reader. He told her very gently that he could not see the birth of any more children in her life. He was concerned that this would sadden her, because it is still quite important for women to have children in his culture. The career woman, however, was relieved, because she had already made a choice not to have any children.

Sometimes there is a problem of scale in interpretation, occasionally with amusing results. Many clairvoyant images come as visions; in Beverly Hills a psychic saw her client receiving a gift of a gold Rolls-Royce. Since this was not as outrageous a prediction in Beverly Hills as it might be elsewhere, the client happily anticipated the arrival of her new car. A couple of weeks later she indeed received it. She was given a charm for her bracelet. A little golden Rolls-Royce.

One of the skills psychics in training learn is appropriate and accurate interpretation. There are techniques for getting clarity on the timing, size, and finally how to express information which is given in a reading in a way which is easily understandable. For example, to determine timing clearly in a reading, the student psychic is taught to 'see' a calendar at the time of the event being viewed; the date it shows will help to fix the date of the expected event.

AURA YOU OR AURA YOU NOT?

What then is it that the psychic reads? Without devices such as horoscopes, cards or palms to rely on, a clairvoyant or psychic has to depend entirely on information from the sixth sense. It is the aura and its contents which tell all to psychics. This aura, or energy field, surrounds each of us. When a client arrives, without saying a word, the aura telegraphs to the psychic information about the past, present condition, thoughts and musings, hopes and fears, and health. It shows what is unfolding in the future and includes both conscious and unconscious thoughts.

Just as the earth itself has a magnetic field which surrounds it, so each of us also has a field. This is the aura. It is composed of two major layers, the first of a sort of white 'fuzz' which usually extends all around the body and up to as much as six inches from its surface. It is amazingly easy to see this aura when looking at someone in a dimly lit room; by allowing the eyes to lose focus slightly, a white glow becomes visible, as if the person is lit from behind. That is what might be called the 'electrical aura'. It may vary slightly in size and intensity, but it looks essentially the same for everyone.

The second aura, however, alters considerably with the state of energy, health and emotional condition. Not as easily seen, this aura extends from three to six feet out from the body. It has colours which change constantly; the differing colours tell the state of attitudes and health. It is similar in appearance to the famous Northern Lights or Aurora Borealis of the polar regions, with its undulating colours. Though few are consciously aware of seeing the auras of others, the colours are obviously perceived on some level, as descriptions of these shades have crept into the language as expressions of mood. When someone is 'feeling blue', the aura is actually tinged with that colour; 'green with envy' produces a dirty green tone, and a 'black mood' has swirling black clouds moving in the auric field. Optimism and love produce a rose hue in the aura, hence the 'rose-glow' of love. The aura around a holy person is gold; the tradition of painting saints and holy people with golden halos around their heads derives from its presence.

REPOSITORY FOR ALL YOUR THOUGHTS

Here in the land of metaphysics, it is accepted that thoughts have form on the energy plane. Thoughts such as mental attitudes, habits and momentary obsessions all get lodged in the aura. Think about something twice a day for a month, and sixty units of those 'thoughts' collect in the aura. While most people are consciously aware of what they think much of the time, we all have things we allow to drift into our minds without realising it. For example, someone who dwells on how bad a job is or how dreadful the boss is will not only arrive at work in a foul mood, but will also make a daily deposit in the aura of those negative thoughts. After a couple of months of this, the aura actually emanates these feelings even without being triggered by thought. By that point the emanations will be felt at work and begin to reflect back in the attitude of co-workers and especially of the boss. No need for a word, the aura sends out everyone's thoughts and feelings.

It is the aura a psychic looks into when giving a reading, and sees thought-forms such as these. A skilled and well-trained psychic will not just parrot back the jumble of attitudes and resentments contained by the energy field, but will translate what is there into potential. Taking the above example, rather than just repeating back the habitual thoughts that work is a bore and the boss hopeless, the reader would suggest remedying the negative mental habits in thinking about work before any constructive changes could be made, and that, unchanged, these attitudes could very well lead to problems.

This is the key to quality in psychic readings. The aura holds the accumulation of thoughts and mental habit patterns which it is the job of the psychic to untangle. The psychic may sense the aura's contents in the form of mental pictures, visions, or by hearing from a guide. No matter how the psychic gets information, it should then be put in a clear manner, and be constructively stated.

Sometimes the greatest contribution a psychic reading can give is the awareness of what is being created through these habitual thought patterns. As the mind roams around, few of us keep track of its wanderings. Habitual thoughts can amass in the aura, shaping 'destiny' without any apparent participation on your part.

I NEVER THOUGHT THAT!

It may be easy to accept the idea that a psychic reads the thoughts and images in the auric field. Yet in readings psychics will make statements about matters clients are quite sure have never been on their minds. If a pure psychic or clairvoyant reading is based only on what is in the aura, and you, as a client, have no recall of having dwelt on the matter at hand, then where did the thought come from?

When the Beverly Hills lady who received a Rolls-Royce – in miniature – heard the prediction, she was surprised and delighted. She said she had never given a thought to receiving a Rolls-Royce of any sort. It was a mystery where the image came from. On reflection she realised that she had indeed thought about it, and almost every time she had passed by a Rolls she amused herself by thinking, 'I'd love to have one of those, I wonder when someone's going to give me one?' And there are plenty of Rolls in Beverly Hills to stimulate that sort of thought!

Another source of images which psychics report in readings comes from our surroundings, from the descriptions and potentials family and friends attribute to us, and attitudes they have about us, all of which sink into our psyches. Most don't even notice when this happens and are so accustomed to nodding and agreeing with others without particularly attending to what they are actually saying that when material of this sort comes up in a reading it is often a surprise.

The aura is like a sponge. It collects whatever is near it. Not only does it carry the reflection of conscious thoughts, desires and emotions, it equally holds the results of unconscious inner chatter, and the variety of ideas absent-mindedly collected from around us. While ideally each of us would benefit from being able to be more selective about what gets deposited in our aura, until this level of control is achieved, a psychic reading will at least help to inform us about what it has accumulated. It is worth remembering that even though you may not have been paying attention to what's been put in your mind, your aura has still been absorbing it, and it will be there for all who see the realm of the sixth sense to read.

WHEN YOU GO

Many people are nervous on their first visit to a psychic. They worry that the psychic will know how untidy they are, or about their unpaid bills. Some are afraid of hearing about illness or loss. These feelings are natural. Letting another person look into your aura, therefore into all your feelings and thoughts, quite rightly makes you feel very vulnerable. So it is essential to give serious thought to the choice of consultant.

Of all of the realms of the kingdom of metaphysics, it is perhaps the psychic realm in which the greatest care must be taken when selecting a reader. Because psychics use no other tool such as a horoscope or cards, they rely totally on the clarity of their ability to perceive information from the sixth sense. If the psychic's own inner mirror is warped in any way, then what they say will be equally warped. If you are easily influenced by what you hear, do not consult a psychic casually or for a quick and cheering fix.

This can be tricky because when consulting a psychic you are at your most open, so information that the psychic gives will 'sink in' more than would an observation made by a friend in casual conversation. If the psychic is well trained and uninfluenced by their own opinions when they work with you, the experience can be enlightening and will give a broader awareness of the patterns in your life.

Psychics, to state an obvious but often forgotten truth, do have individual personalities; you will get on better with some than with others. Psychics also have different styles in the way they work and this working style is an extension of their personality. The quality of 'click' between you is called rapport. An easy connection not only makes for a feeling of comfort and security, it makes it easier for you to open up and for the psychic to read you.

TYPES OF PSYCHICS

Pleaser Says what you want to hear, doesn't challenge too much, reassures, may give constructive advice, you feel great when you leave; low percentage of long-term accuracy.

Provoker Challenges in areas where you are unsure, may put things in an irritating fashion, makes you question, may suggest alternative action; not good if you are already insecure, but can give feeling of stimulation and challenge; usually fairly accurate.

Addictor Like the pleaser, says what you want to hear, but never tells enough so as to give secure feeling in making decisions, can create dependence; not particularly accurate; focuses on short term.

Judge Criticises what you do and how you do it, can create feeling of dependence or need for approval, takes 'parent' role; can encourage or erode independence; sometimes quite accurate as does not try to please.

Psycho Often has a personally disturbed background; uses psychic abilities to gain power over clients, uses intuition to see weak spots and create feeling of dependence; accuracy very spotty.

Pro Trained to observe without influence of personal opinions; encourages in what is perceived as beneficial, gently calls attention to situations which may not prove to be so; discourages dependence; very accurate.

COLD READINGS

While there is a wide variety of methods used by legitimate psychics, there is also one utilised by fraudulent practitioners. The 'cold reading' is a technique employed by the unscrupulous who use deduction instead of psychic powers to give a reading. Scientists who dedicate their work to disproving that the sixth sense exists cite the use of this technique as evidence that all psychic powers are rubbish, which is perhaps a slight overstatement. The method, as fascinating as it is important to know about, is not only used by scientists unsympathetic to the psychic realm, it is employed by carnival readers as well. The reader will take note of characteristics enough to get the reading started by observing how well, expensively, or tidily dressed a client is, the presence of a wedding ring, other jewellery, as well as behaviour and gestures. For example, if the client's shoes are expensive but need polishing and reheeling, the reader would venture a statement the client likes good things and to live well, longs to be looked after by someone, and tends to put things off. As the client responds to initial statements, the reader will adjust further ones.

FINDING AND SELECTING A CONSULTANT

As with all the areas of the metaphysical realm, the easiest way to find a psychic is to ask friends. Many will have quite passionate opinions about their psychics. Be careful not to let friends' enthusiasm sweep personal assessment away. While a friend may thrive on a judgmental psychic's gaze, you may be the sort who withers at the smallest criticism. Another friend may go to consult a psychic once a month, but you may not like the idea of this sort of dependence. Listen, then, to friends' suggestions, but also take note of the friend's character as well.

If no friends can come up with suggestions, metaphysical centres usually have psychics on the staff who see clients. By describing the style of reading you prefer, the staff can suggest someone who might mesh nicely with your needs. Many psychics advertise in magazines as well.

No matter what the source of the referral, ask the fee for a session when making an appointment. A few psychics do not charge at all, some request a donation, but most have fixed fees, especially if they are professionals, that is they actually make their living from their consulting work. The fee should be within the range of most professional consultants in your community, about the same as a private doctor or a solicitor would be paid for an hour of their time.

There are those who object to paying for a session with a psychic, feeling that the ability is a gift, and one from the spiritual realm, so they believe such a gift should be given for free. There are also some psychics who agree with this. But as very few psychics are independently wealthy, most of them do rely on their income from their work for a living. They have taken the time and made the effort to develop their gift into a reliable skill from which the client benefits. It is fair they be compensated for this.

WHAT TO ASK

As with all the areas of the sixth sense, the visit will be more beneficial if some time is taken beforehand to organise thoughts and clarify questions. For example, if a relationship is in a difficult period, is it reassurance that is desired, or would an analysis of the problems which are the source of the situation be useful? Knowing what information is wanted beforehand will give more satisfactory results.

Even though you may not get around to actually asking your questions, they will be part of the thoughts in your aura when you walk in. Before the session starts, enquire when to ask any questions you do have. Some psychics do not like to be disturbed while they are working, but will answer questions at the end of the session, others will want to know at the start if there is anything special on your mind.

As with all readings, it is worthwhile to tape-record the session. Some psychics do not like the practice, others prefer it; do ask. It is very difficult later to recall everything that has been said. If the session was not recorded, then take notes immediately afterwards in as much detail as you can remember, whether you like or agree with what was said or not; in order to review the session, a full record is necessary.

THE SESSION'S NOT OVER WHEN IT'S OVER

Ideally the session will have been taped. Even if it was not, afterwards it is important to evaluate the information given. If possible do this before discussing the session with anyone. Because of the 'magical' quality of the psychic realm, it is easy to turn psychic predictions into a sort of revealed truth. If this is done without taking time to reflect seriously on the content of the reading, then it is easy to let the psychic make decisions about your life for you.

The best result is not necessarily that you liked everything said. Often psychics will let us in on little secrets from the depths of our psyches that our conscious minds have been hiding from us. And sometimes these are facts we may not be too pleased to hear; but still they ring true. If everything seemed completely positive, it is likely the psychic was a 'Pleaser'. While this sort of reading results in a great feeling temporarily, it gives no incisive views on life. If after the session you felt small and powerless, it is likely the psychic was 'Judgemental', one who will make you work to please – them! If you feel peculiar and disoriented after the session, you may have encountered a mentally disturbed psychic, whose glimpses into your psyche are from their own warped vision. It is essential to think if you wish to accept as true the things the psychic has said, about you, your character, your future. This would be vital in the last case mentioned. If you're unfamiliar with the realm of the sixth sense, that is all the more reason to be very careful in assessing a reader's interpretation.

No psychic will be correct in everything they say. Even those who are able to act as the clearest of mirrors still must contend with elements such as the free will of others altering the future they see unfolding; a change of mind on the part of another can create a change of 'destiny'. Often clients will find that statements about the past and predictions concerning the near future are correct, so they rely on longer-range predictions to be equally precise.

The further in the future the date of a prediction, the less accurate it will be likely to be; there is more time for events to occur which would alter the course of what has been predicted. In addition, psychics themselves have particular areas in which they are more accurate and others where they are less so. Unless familiar with which areas are a particular psychic's strength, it is wise not to rely completely on any prediction.

The reading is not over until you have evaluated it both intellectually and reflected on your feelings about what you have been told. It is worth while to divide the information given into two categories: one of statements which make sense and are easily acceptable, and one of those about which there are some reservations. The presence of some impressive elements in a reading is not enough to indicate that everything said should be accepted. And of course, if *anything* stated was frightening, place it immediately in a suspect category, not to be accepted until it is reviewed and discussed with a trusted friend.

Ideally a reading will result in your feeling both optimistic, that goals are possible, and challenged, aware of the matters which must be dealt with before those changes can take place.

THE RIGHT READER

It may take a few trial visits to psychics to find one who is comfortable. Some find they like different ones for different sorts of information. One may be better at looking at personal life, another better at business. Shop around, get experience, ask questions. If you liked a psychic enough to return but found not everything came out as predicted, ask if the psychic can explain why. This is the way to learn about the psychic world; and you may equally learn something about yourself.

For those who spend the majority of their time occupied with the demands of family, job and resources, a visit to the realm of clairvoyants and psychics can broaden a world narrowed by the pressures of daily life. Others are given a new perspective on problems and situations which may have seemed unmanageable. However, the greatest gift offered by this realm is a clearer image of how each of us takes part in shaping our own future and the knowledge of how to enhance it as it unfolds.

9

Spiritualism and Channelling

At one time, life in the realm of the spirits was simple: there was just the local medium and her spirit guide with messages from the dear departed. Now the spirit world is booming and there is a confusion of beings, seen and unseen, both here in the physical world and on 'the other side'. Spiritualists, the oldtimers of this world, have been joined recently by channellers, who add a new angle to otherworldly conversations. Discover whereabouts is home to the spirited beings channelled today. Wander the byways of these realms and learn who mediums and channels speak to, how to evaluate them and their translucent associates and to recognise the domain's denizens – even the invisible ones.

(I) SPIRITUALISM

A SPIRITED DISCUSSION

The world of psychics and mediums divides itself tidily into two parts. Psychics or clairvoyants, to whom you've already been introduced in Chapter 8, delve into the aura to get their information. Mediums or channels use the information not from the aura, but from beings in the realm of the sixth sense.

In that kingdom we acknowledge that there is life beyond the physical plane. The beings we call ghosts are only one of several types of entities from that plane; it has many

116

different levels and a variety of types of residents. There are several names for the place that ghosts and their colleagues call home, but the easiest term for those of us on this side of the border is 'the other side'.

Ghosts or spirits are probably the most familiar of beings on the other side. Ghosts who do nothing else but haunt houses are treated in the next chapter. They and their invisible cousins have quite different careers from those you will meet in this chapter. They have some traits in common, however. Because they are still emotionally attached to the earth, they live in the part of the other side closest to it and for this reason are easiest for us to see. Some ghosts do not yet realise they are dead, and are, needless to say, confused. While ghosts can make an impressive appearance, with behaviour such as passing through solid walls, floating in mid-air, moaning, clanking and even speaking, they are really not the most reliable sources of accurate information from the other side.

There are other residents who have a quieter demeanour than their ghostly relations. Some are beings who, like ghosts, were once alive here on earth. When they died, unlike ghosts, they made a conscious decision to remain connected with the earth plane, to work as supporters and advisors to us still here on earth. Having had a spiritual orientation in life, they continue to dedicate themselves to helping others after casting off the physical body. Most religious traditions speak of 'saints', great beings who have passed on, to whom the faithful pray for assistance and wisdom, and who assist in miracles and healing.

Also living in this realm are beings who have never been embodied on the earth's physical plane. Not 'extra-terrestrials' in the sense of being entities from other planets or other solar systems, these beings are from other planes rather than other planets. They come as guides for this planet and try to foster wisdom in its residents and keep some kind of order.

It may sound as if the 'other side' is crowded. Here on earth we are accustomed to thinking of just one plane of existence – ours. But the other side has many, many levels, on which beings of different sorts live.

Just as in any major city it is possible to visit various neighbourhoods, each unique in its residents, appearance and feeling, the other side has distinct areas too. These regions are separated not by geographical location, but by the factor which differentiates areas on the other side, the quality of the energy. More spiritually orientated beings are composed of substance more refined than ones whose dominant energies are emotional and personally orientated. Those who are still strongly attached to the earth and therefore have a denser energy gather together, while beings with a finer energy will find themselves in their own region of the realm.

MEDIUMS AND CHANNELS – WHO'S WHO

Mediums have long been associated with table tilting, mysterious rappings, and hands appearing out of the dark. While ghosts have been part of the landscape as long as anyone can remember, it was only with the advent of spiritualism in the nineteenth century that ghosts were actually invited to come for a chat.

Spiritualists aim to demonstrate that there is life after death by communicating with the departed. This communication takes place in private consultations or in group sessions. The agent through whom the departed speaks is called a medium, and the session a seance.

Interest sprang up in contacting spirits at about the same time in both the UK and the USA, although the USA gets credit for the start of modern spiritualism. It began in rural New York state; the Fox family had moved into their home, already known to be haunted, the previous year. On 31 March 1848, the three Fox sisters began a conversation with the spirit world which shows no signs of ending even today. The household ghost had been rattling around regularly, but that night, instead of just letting their ghost make aimless taps, they demanded that it respond to their questions. Starting simply, the Fox sisters asked it to rap out their ages. From this, a dialogue with their Mr Splitfoot, as their ghost was called, flourished. Eventually, their conversations with the other side were taken on the stage and Margaret, Kate and Leah Fox became the rock stars of their time.

The spiritualist phenomenon spread rapidly over America and across the Atlantic. Mediums became media events. The most famous, impressive, and by most accounts, legitimate, medium was a Scots-born American called Daniel Douglas Home. By 1868 he had established himself in England and Europe as an astonishing, as well as charming, medium. His feats were showstoppers; disembodied hands appeared in mid-air, an accordion played without any hands at all. These events took place in well-lit rooms and he was never discredited as employing tricks in creating his effects.

As well known by the public as mediums became, often their control, the being from the other side who acted as the link with the spirit world, became even more famous. One such case was the beautiful medium Florence Cook, whose spirit control was the equally stunning (and equally often photographed) Katie King, who shimmered in white robes during seances by Cook.

As the result of scientific interest in the 1880s there were organised Societies for Psychical Research in England, in 1882, and in America in 1885. At that time spiritualism was taken as a very serious phenomenon, and legitimate scientists studied the better-known mediums in the hope of understanding the powers they used.

In the later stages of the fashion for mediums, a particularly fascinating struggle took place between two notable and charismatic characters. Sir Arthur Conan Doyle, famous as the creator of Sherlock Holmes, was a passionate spiritualist. He spoke, wrote and lectured on the subject. His counterpart was the magician Harry Houdini, who was equally passionate on the subject of fraud in the spiritualist world. Houdini did not object to the concept of speaking to the spirit world itself, as is witnessed by the fact that before his death he arranged a code he would use in trying to communicate to his wife, if that were indeed possible, from the other side. (Several seances were conducted, though Mrs Houdini did acknowledge that she had received the agreed-upon message, she would not accept that it was her husband's spirit.) What Houdini did object to was the misuse of spiritualist techniques to take advantage of gullible members of the public, still an issue today. Conan Doyle and Houdini debated in public, wrote books, each carrying his banner with vigour, neither ever really winning his point.

The craze for spiritualism began to wane in the 1920s. Interest in it has never disappeared entirely and there are still mediums today who catch the public eye. Though there are a number who are popular and highly visible, a particularly fascinating one in England is Rosemary Brown, known for receiving the piano works of long-dead composers.

The spiritualist societies continue and the tradition of mediumship still thrives in the UK. These groups train mediums, and it is still possible to visit a group seance at a spiritualist group, or to have a private consultation with a medium.

WHEN YOU GO

Some go to consult a medium because they wish to be in contact with a friend or relative who has died. Others go because they want to use the information given by the medium's 'spirit control' as psychic guidance. The atmosphere of a seance and an assurance that there is life beyond death is appealing for some.

It is not difficult to find a place to go; many towns have spiritualist associations. If you are unfamiliar with the spirit realm, it is best to start by contacting an organisation where the mediums have been trained properly.

WHAT THE SPIRITS CAN TELL YOU

For those unaccustomed to conversing with the spirit world, it may seem a bit peculiar at first to communicate with the deceased, to have questions answered, and even to receive advice from them.

A group seance is done in the most friendly and natural fashion. Perhaps disappointingly, very few spiritualists are anything but warm and charming. At the start, the group will gather and may ask for divine guidance and protection for the seance. The medium will sit quietly for a moment, as will the group. He or she may go into a trance, or simply begin to speak. Usually the medium's own spirit guide, or 'control', will speak first. Often this will be a deceased relative of the medium; it may start with a message for the group, or answer queries. Then the focus of the seance will turn to the group and, speaking via the medium, either the control or a departed friend or family member will give messages to members of the audience. Sometimes these seem meaningless to the assembly, but will have pertinence to the individual. Though rarely revealing where the stolen jewels or the final copy of the will were hidden, these messages seem intended to reassure those still on this plane that things are not bad at all for those on the other side. Often this can be deeply touching and there may be tears shed at this point in the seance.

Messages having been given, the floor will be opened for questions from the audience. Again, this will rarely be an exercise in philosophy, but rather questions about ordinary day-to-day issues such as whether to get tougher with a child about studying or if it is wise to put the house up for sale.

While each group will have its own format, this is a fair guide of what to expect. Nice people, comfy atmosphere and friendly chats with the dead. Once you become accustomed to it, it all seems perfectly natural.

An individual session takes place in a quiet location. You may wish to be in touch with a person who has recently passed over or just ask questions. Normally the medium will sit quietly and may say a prayer in preparation. The session will usually start with a statement from the medium's spirit control, perhaps some advice and an opportunity to ask any questions of a general nature. Or it may go immediately to waiting entities, not necessarily the one you had in mind to see, but possibly relatives such as grandparents or others who have been dead for some time. They will usually give some words of warmth and comfort. They may say they have been looking after you, they may recount a recent event where there was a decision to make, or where you were alerted to a danger by your guardian angel in the form of that departed loved one.

On some occasions it is not possible to talk to the recently dead, especially if they died suddenly or in confusion. When this is the case, the individual is not available because of being disorientated and will be looked after by guides.

THE LADY WHOSE MOTHER APOLOGISED

Other times a spirit may come forward without being bidden. In a private seance, a woman was surprised when she was told her mother had a message for her. Her mother had died very recently, but she had spent a good deal of time with her and had plenty of time to say her goodbyes. The past several years had been occupied in attending to her mother, who had become increasingly senile and difficult. Her mother came because she wished to apologise for being such a burden, asked forgiveness and promised to help her from the other side.

SPIRIT RELIABILITY

The obvious question is how accurate the information received in a seance is. Fortunately, what is said is rarely the sort of stuff on which the winning or losing of fortunes is based. The focus of queries tends to be more personal and more homely; but still one wonders how much trust should be placed in statements such as, 'Do not sell your home until May', when the plan had been to put it up for sale tomorrow.

Aside from the normal clear-minded assessment of what's been said, the best guide is experience. It is easy to empower a disembodied voice, especially if it seems to give good suggestions. But not all spirits are good at giving advice about all things. It helps to learn what sort of guidance can be trusted. Some spirits seem to have connections in high places and give very accurate guidance, others are spotty indeed. With time it is possible to learn what is reliable.

For example, a woman, a medium herself, received conflicting advice from two relatives who had passed on. She had to make a decision about signing a legal document involving a large sum of money. Seeking guidance, her late aunt told her to sign it, as it would benefit her, but her late father advised her not to. Confusing counsel from the spirits! In this case she didn't have to puzzle too much what to do. When he was alive, her father was not known as a financial expert; he appeared not to have got any wiser on the other side.

SPIRITUAL SENSATIONALISM

After having gotten accustomed to the idea of talking to someone without a body, it may be necessary to get accustomed to the idea of gifts being left behind. When spirits leave objects behind, they are not usually of value, though they may have significance to the spirit or the recipient. Here we enter the land of spiritual phenomena, a risky area indeed for the uninformed. The manifestation of physical items, called in the spiritualist world 'apports', can be persuasive; it can also indicate fraud. The basic rule to apply is the more sensational, or valuable, the items produced, the more wary to be.

Individual evaluation is the only answer here. Over the

ages spiritual teachers have been known to create, or manifest, and give to followers and devotees tokens, and gifts of value. In most religions, manifestation of this sort is considered to be miraculous. But in the hands of the less spiritually orientated, they can equally be used to persuade the vulnerable and gullible. If you encounter a spiritualist setting where there is impressive manifestation occurring, be watchful for the following conditions:

· Demands for money, a single large sum or repeated sums.
· Using the 'manifestation' to prove the presence of a high being.
· Demands for your time, to bring other people, commit yourself to classes, all to benefit spiritual progress.

It is not unknown for high spiritual teachers to present their students with manifested gifts. Perhaps the ability to discriminate between the genuine and the fraudulent is a vital point of transition in personal spiritual progress.

(II) CHANNELLING

TUNING INTO THE RIGHT CHANNEL

It isn't only in television that more channels have been appearing. The spiritualist world has a whole new region, similar in principle, but with some differing elements; it is called channelling.

Amongst metaphysical enthusiasts, channelling is enjoying a vogue. Those who would never consider attending a seance at the local spiritualist society have been introduced to conversations with the other side through channelling. Spiritualism and channelling are fundamentally the same thing – the process in which a being who is not physically embodied speaks through one who is. The variations are subtle, and are probably a good statement of the change in attitude and development of interest towards the metaphysical realm. In the early 1800s when spiritualism first came to light, the purpose was to prove that life existed after physical death. Now, nearly 200 years later, with channelling, there is no longer a question of the need for proof but rather a philosophical interest in learning about the various non-physical planes, and in deriving wisdom from the entities who dwell on them. While the beings who appear through channelled means do deal with personal matters, conversations are more orientated towards gaining an understanding of life.

WHAT IS ON THIS CHANNEL?

As was the case when spiritualism first appeared, there has been sensationalism and accusations of fraud. It doesn't make sense to judge all of the practitioners of channelling as bad because some have gained a great deal of notoriety and wealth as the result of their activities.

There are a number of theories about what actually occurs when channelling happens. Some insist it is indeed a separate being who comes from another plane to speak to us on this one. Others insist that it is an aspect of the channeller's own 'higher self', the wiser, more divinely connected part which we could all experience if we were willing to get our conscious minds out of the way. There are, of course, those who insist it is all a made-up show and is of entertainment value only.

At its best, channelling offers an opportunity to benefit from the wisdom of a being who resides in a world with a wider view than ours. Channelling seems to maintain as its focus a philosophical understanding of even life's most mundane problems. It could reasonably be called the psychotherapy of the metaphysical realm, as not only are events and situations considered but the motivation behind them as well. For example, a woman brought to a session the problem of someone with whom she simply did not get on. She asked in the session how to deal with the situation, understand her better, to be more generous of nature. She was told it really was not her problem, that the other was indeed unstable and jealous and there was no reason to continue the relationship. In addition she was told that the issue derived from a previous life where the situation had been similar and it would thus be wise to make a formal break so as not to continue the drama into future lives.

Often public channelling sessions are rather more like philosophical discourses. As with Sunday sermons, the range of quality of these is wide and seems to depend on the entity who is being channelled. This brings up the major question in the realm of channelling: How to evaluate what you can't see.

HOW DO YOU TELL WHAT'S GOOD?

There are two things to attend to. The first is your response to what you hear. Does it give you a feeling of hopefulness about life, is it empowering and does it give a view which helps to understand and resolve conflicts? Or does it give a sense of being helpless, needing to return for more information, not being able to cope? It is easy to empower someone invisible who pronounces philosophical profundities. But the bottom line, as they say in Hollywood, is whether those profundities help you in getting on with life.

The other form of assessment is to look at the person who is channelling. In the early days of spiritualism, when the spirits who were being channelled were once humans with no pretensions to being great teachers, anyone who had natural gifts as an intuitive and was properly trained could act as a medium. In channelling beings from higher levels, the channel must be trained, almost like an athlete, to be able to bring through the intensity of energy of more powerful beings.

As with all areas in the land of the metaphysical, the only person who can assess the value of who and what you hear is you. Here are a few guidelines:

Character Take a look at the channel as an individual. This is the best clue to the level of energy coming through. Very simply put, like an electric wire, the channel can

126

bear only the energy they have the capacity for. If in daily life the channel has an unkind nature, uninspiring ethics, questionable finances, then the level of energy is likely to be equally constricted. Channels are human beings, with human frailties, so do not expect perfection, but if the dissonance between the wisdom of the purported entity and the channel's everyday behaviour is great, there may be reason to question. Sophistication, however, is no measure, as there are many fine channels who are simple, humble individuals.

Money While all professionals deserve to be paid, consider if the amount requested as fees for private consultations and workshops is reasonable in terms of your community's standards. Are you asked to make additional contributions or engage in business deals? Query this!

Omniscience Does the entity claim to know your mind better than you do? Does it discuss your 'fate', 'soul mate', or anything else which takes destiny out of your hands?

WHAT YOU'VE BEEN TOLD – WHEN YOU GO

One of the most mystifying elements in a group or private channelling session is that you are not talking to the person with whom you are communicating. Until you become accustomed to it, it seems peculiar to have the body of one, but the presence of another. This is daunting indeed for the inexperienced, and there is a risk to be taken into account as well.

When the session begins, the channel will probably enter a trance. A state rather like self-induced hypnosis, the trance enables the channel to 'step aside' and allow the entity who is being channelled to come through. The intensity of the trance varies from a light trance where the channeller is capable of making personal asides whilst doing the channelling to a state of profound unconsciousness where the body is left apparently empty so that the being who is coming through may take up temporary residence.

While listening, speaking and asking questions during the

session, remember you are not speaking to the person sitting in the chair. Perhaps because you cannot see the speaker it is easy to empower this invisible being. Therefore it is important to ask questions the moment they come up and respond quickly to anything said which is troubling at once. It won't be possible to do it when the session is over as you might with a psychic or astrologer, because the entity to whom you were speaking will be gone. And the channel can't be responsible for what has been said either.

DO IT YOURSELF?

Is there anyone who made it through their teenage years without having sat giggling with friends at the Ouija board while watching as letter by letter the answers to the group's questions were spelled out? Yet, as light-hearted as these early forays into the other side may have been, for many they ended with both a sense of respect for the power of the realm and a not inappropriate fear of unsupervised experimentation.

This is not the safest of areas of the metaphysical kingdom to set out as a Do-It-Yourselfer. As participation in this realm requires opening up the psyche to other beings, even when doing something as apparently harmless as the Ouija board, there really is nothing that can be done safely without supervision and some instruction.

We forget that in addition to the perfectly fine people who die there are also those who weren't especially wonderful when they were alive who have gone on to be not very nice spirits. They live in what might be called the slums of the other side. Taking part in any of the seemingly playful aspects of this realm, such as automatic writing, the Ouija board, or trying your hand at mediumship or channelling, is an open invitation to any passing entity. If you are a natural intuitive, or very impressionable, it is possible that the being attracted will not be the sort you would have invited into your home when it was alive, and it may be difficult to get rid of the 'visitor' when you want to. This happened to one teenage experimenter when, unable to resist trying with automatic writing, her hand was guided across the paper, writing words which were revealed to her only as they appeared. Eventually she grew tired of her attempts and told her friends she had enough and was finished. A voice audible to all said, 'No you're not!' Her spirit was not willing to go home. Training teaches you how to glide past these slums to invite a more refined type of entity to come to call and how to make sure they leave when the session is over.

OTHERWORLDLY INVITATION

Explorations of the other side and its residents can be a great adventure. This realm of the sixth sense can be one of the most touching and philosophically satisfying when contact is made with departed loved ones and there comes a sense of life beyond our own mundane reality. By proceeding with intelligence and caution, and evaluating what you hear, every experience will enhance your awareness.

The opportunity to learn from high beings who share gifts of wisdom and understanding can enhance life in innumerable ways. Being able to receive their guidance and extended perspective can only benefit you and those in your world.

In returning to daily activities you may find your experiences with the other side has given you a gift – a richer sense of life, deeper understanding of others, greater patience and a considerably expanded view of reality.

10

Ghosts and Spirits

A haunted house! Evocative and thrilling words. Of all of the areas of the sixth sense, this is perhaps the most exciting, and frightening. The realm of ghosts and spirits may be the most confusing as well. Exploring it is an adventure, populated as it is with a wide variety of sorts of beings: the souls of humans who have died, poltergeists, unruly spirits, nature spirits and devas. Some are benevolent; some just noisy and difficult; some menacing.

WHERE GHOSTS LIVE

All the ghostly beings dwell on the plane above the physical, usually called the astral plane. It coexists with our own physical plane, and is composed of a substance which is finer than that of the physical world. This is why ghosts and spirits can pass through apparently solid matter, such as closed doors and walls. A fair comparison would be to suggest that the astral plane is like very fine sand which would pass easily through a sieve; the matter of our plane is like small pebbles, too coarse to pass through the same screen.

VOCABULARY

Soul The portion of an individual which lives on after physical death. This portion carries elements of character.

Astral plane The plane next above our physical plane, in which beings who have lost their bodies, such as ghosts, or who have never had physical bodies, such as spirits, exist.

Ghost The disembodied soul of an individual who has died but has remained near the earth plane.

Spirit Usually used interchangeably with ghost; may also mean a poltergeist or nature spirit.

Poltergeist The word is from the German meaning noisy spirit. Disruptive energy, the appearance of which is usually connected to a specific individual, not a place. Unlike a ghost, not the spirit of a once-living person. Activities are usually stimulated by strong emotions.

Elf, pixie, fairy Spirit beings living in nature, associated with plants, trees, earth, minerals.

Nature spirit (elemental) Beings who rule the world of the elements of nature. Each element has its own individual type of creature:

> **undine** – water elemental
> **zephyr** or **sylph** – wind elemental
> **salamander** – fire elemental
> **gnome** – earth elemental

Exorcism The process of removing an unwelcome non-physical being from either a place or from a person. Performed by a trained individual, most religions, including the Christian one, have such rituals.

GHOSTLY ORIGINS

The beings of this plane come from two distinctly different origins. Ghosts are the disembodied souls of former human beings. They are also often called spirits as well, though for our purposes here we will reserve the word spirit for the remainder of the residents of this realm, which can be classified as poltergeists, nature spirits and fairy beings.

Ghosts probably get the most attention of all the residents of this realm. Nothing is more fun than sitting around a fire hearing tales of ghosts, and a resident ghost may even enhance the resale value of an old house. Everyone who stays in a place reputed to be 'haunted' both hopes and fears they will actually get to see the ghostly tenant.

Many wonder how a ghost got where it is in the first place. Ghosts tend to reside either in the place where they lived, or where they died. Because ghosts were once human beings, they have emotions and attachments as we all do. Most people when they die are able to release those strong feelings as they leave the physical body. It appears that the souls who stay connected with the physical plane and become ghosts do so because they did not complete that process and are kept attached because of an intense emotional connection of which they cannot rid themselves. The emotion comes either as the result of an event during the life which remained unresolved, or because of the manner in which the individual died. The following are examples of situations of this sort.

GHOST STORIES

In a very old house in the Home Counties, the young lady of the house was consistently bothered by a cold chill when she reached the top of the stairs. No one else was troubled by this. Puzzled, she asked a visiting friend who was a psychic if she could tell her anything about this peculiar situation. Standing in the spot where her hostess felt the chill, the psychic sensed the presence of a former lady of the house. It appeared she had lost her baby in childbirth and could have no more. The crib of the lost child had been stored in the attic directly overhead at the top of the stairs. She haunted that spot, mourning her lost child and the loss of motherhood. When the new lady of the house, young enough to have children of her own, was near that spot the former resident's sigh of sadness was felt as a cold chill. After the ghost had been recognised, the present lady of the house was no longer troubled.

In a house in Wiltshire, an officer stares out of the window longing to rejoin his men who are fighting. They are fighting the Civil War and he is in the room where he died, hundreds of years ago, where he was taken to be looked after when he was injured. Ever since, he has gazed out of that window, unaware of the passage of time or that all his men have long since passed on.

Both these souls had strong emotions which chained them to the places they were haunting. The lady lived many years after she lost her child, but was never freed of her sadness, unreleased even after she died. The officer stayed in the spot where his life ended, still longing to return to his men.

WHY GHOSTS CLANK

Jokes abound about ghosts who walk around with their heads under their arms, ghosts who moan and ghosts who clank chains. The fact is individuals who die unresolved deaths, such as from being beheaded, chained in a dungeon, or more likely in today's world, in an unexpected way such as an auto crash, all share the intense unresolved emotion at the time of their death. Ghosts still rattling around from deaths hundreds of years ago may merely be confused about the fact they actually are dead. Ghosts of individuals who were beheaded or the like often want to get even with the individual who ordered the execution. Because there is not the same firm concept of time on the astral, the ghostly, plane as we have on our own, ghosts are not aware of the passing of the years and have no conception that they have been hanging about longing for retribution for several hundred years. These extended cases are rare, however.

In the case of most deaths, the time it takes to resolve

this longing is not great. Over the ages, in situations where individuals have died unexpectedly, whether by accident or sudden illness, reports of 'visits' by the deceased or loved ones have been common. These goodbye calls are part of the process of letting go of those emotional ties in a manner which frees the soul to move on. Sometimes in the case of particularly tragic deaths, the soul itself will stay watching over loved ones until they have recovered enough to cope and get on with life. Normally, the time this process takes ranges from perhaps six months to a year. During this time there may be a feeling of the presence of the departed. When those emotional ties have finally been released, the soul then departs this plane. It is worth noting that most cultures and major religions have a formal mourning period of a year, the time during which those emotional links are gradually diminished through mourning rituals.

A GHOST'S POINT OF VIEW

Ghosts are attached by emotion to a place. To understand how this works, it may be easier to look at the world from a ghost's point of view. On the astral plane time is not the same as it is for us. The physical body and the logically reasoning mind are lost with the death of the body. The astral plane is dominated by desire. In the case of a ghost, it is desire, created by unresolved emotions, which keep it connected to this, the plane nearest the earth plane. It sees us about as dimly as we see it. A ghost responds to two types of beings: highly emotional persons or psychic ones. Both of these types of energy penetrate the astral realm, and can connect more easily with the plane on which the ghost lives.

As ghosts live on the astral plane, it is through this plane that it is easiest for them to make their actions felt. Not being connected with the physical plane, ghosts are only rarely able to hurl vases around rooms or lift tables. Their home, the astral plane, is nearer in energy to what we use as electricity on our physical plane. These days, ghosts often try to communicate by brightening or dimming lights, or affecting other electrical appliances, such as turning on and off radios, record players and similar appliances. The following is an example.

A news reporter in America was fascinated with an unsolved murder. The victim was a young woman. Committed in the 1940s, this sensational murder had been the subject of several movies. No one had found out who committed the murder, and the reporter spent his spare time interviewing the police and others who had been involved at the time, trying to crack the case. As he became more intensely absorbed, he found his answering machine would have strange, unintelligible messages on it, and his stereo turned itself on and off as he sat in the room well away from it. The more time he spent on the case, the more phenomena of this sort occurred. A sceptical hard-bitten journalist, it was difficult for him to accept the obvious conclusion, that the victim was trying to get in touch with him. Nevertheless, he found no other explanation for these events.

WHO CAN TALK TO GHOSTS

When someone is emotionally overwrought, the feelings act as a magnet to a ghost, who is drawn by the intensity of energy from that person. A ghost will often try to communicate through an individual of this sort.

An individual with psychic powers will equally draw the attention of the ghosts, in the same magnetic way. A psychic, particularly if properly trained, can act as a mediator with a ghost and help it to understand that the resolution or the revenge which it has been seeking for so many years is unlikely to occur and that all the other members of the cast of his drama have long since died. Many ghosts continue to hang around only because no one has ever 'spoken' to them. They are just confused and need a little guidance. When they understand the situation, they will often go quietly on their way. Supernatural psychotherapy!

NASTY GHOSTS

Some ghosts are not such benevolently confused beings. In rare cases they are downright nasty. Nasty ghosts were usually pretty dreadful people when they were alive, and may have got worse having lost the constraints the physical plane put on them. These beings have no conscience about moving uninvited into someone's house, or body even.

The stuff of Gothic horror novels and movies, this sort of ghost can play havoc with lives. Where a ghost is attracted to an emotional situation which allows it to feed off the energy of living beings, this may be the source of the vampire legend. Attracted to weak or disturbed personalities, where it can take over the body without much resistance, it displaces the soul of the original resident.

A ghost of this type will cause physical discomfort and emotional distress to those who live in 'its' residence and to those who come to visit. It feeds off their energy and is a danger to those of a delicate psychological constitution.

GHOST FIXERS

As ghosts have been around for quite some time, so have those who sort out ghosts. Most cultures have a 'ghost specialist', someone who is trained to deal with the unpleasant type of ghost. They were called shaman, witch doctor or medicine man in ancient cultures, and the tradition continues in most religions. Christian churches have priests specially assigned to this task. The title used has been made legend by the Hollywood movie, *The Exorcist*. Whatever the religious background, all of these individuals are trained by their predecessors and use ancient rituals to accomplish their goals of ridding a person or a location of a ghost.

While most ghosts make themselves benign house guests, the fact is ghosts do live on the highly emotionally energised astral plane. If they are of a very unpleasant nature, they can influence the emotions of those who try to deal with them and be equally unpleasant to have around. It still occurs today where in serious cases an expert will be needed to do some 'ghost-busting'.

NOT QUITE GHOSTS – POLTERGEISTS

Many people think of dishes and pots being hurled around the room when the word ghost is mentioned. The disturbing phenomena they are thinking of are not usually the result of ghosts, but of poltergeists, the noisy and troublesome members of the spirit world.

Believed to have a different origin than ghosts, who are souls of human beings who have died, poltergeists seem to appear as the result of a particular individual being in a specific location. While ghostly hauntings may go on in the same way over centuries, poltergeist activity seems to appear with sudden intensity, continue for perhaps some months, and then cease. A poltergeist may not be a 'being' in the same way as other beings discussed here are, but may rather be a temporary collection of energies.

Poltergeist is a German word which means noisy spirit. It is the noise, in fact, that initially differentiates poltergeists from ghosts. While ghosts may sigh and clank and rattle, poltergeists pound walls, make the sound of booms and explosions which would seem enough to shake a house down. Famous for moving objects and furniture around, and even starting fires, poltergeist visitations are dreaded. They also seem to be able to 'take' objects away from the physical plane, actually making them disappear, and then return them.

Studies of poltergeist activity done by psychologists have shown that they most often appear when emotions are at a very intense peak, such as when a resident of a house is deeply upset, or when there is an adolescent present.

Traditional exorcisms of the sort which are effective with ghosts seem not to have much effect on poltergeists. The activity normally ceases, however, often of its own accord, after a period of months.

ELEMENTALS AND DEVAS – SPIRITS OF NATURE

Less well known than ghosts or even than naughty poltergeists are the nature spirits – the beings who rule the elements of nature, earth, fire and water – and devas, who reign over all the species of plants. The elementals of earth are called gnomes; of water, undines; of air, zephyrs or sylphs; and of fire, salamanders. Though we sometimes use the words which describe these creatures, few of us are aware that these terms define actual beings. Perhaps the lack of familiarity with these beings illustrates the loss of connection with nature which reflects a major crisis of our time.

The nature spirits are individual beings, ruled over by an overseeing spirit being in each kingdom. People who live in the country or who make an effort to maintain their contact with nature often have a friendly sense of these beings.

ELEMENTARY ELEMENTALS

You may have seen elementals yourself without realising it. Many people who consider themselves to have no psychic vision can, nevertheless, easily see air elementals on sunlit days. Looking into the sky, the eye sees what appears to be countless little lights darting around. Those are the zephyrs or sylphs. Gathered together, they become breezes; collected in agitation they become windstorms and hurricanes.

The elementals of the water, the undines, can be spotted playing among flowing water in rivers, the ocean, or even in city fountains. The relaxing sound of water flowing is the happy chatter of the undines. Their power is apparent to anyone who has witnessed a stormy sea.

A fireplace may afford a view of salamanders, the fiery sprites whose lively antics catch the eye of animals in a room as well as of people. When excited, as in a bonfire on Guy Fawkes Day, the salamanders leap high in the air and are especially easy to spot.

Gnomes, the elementals of earth, are perhaps best known as fairy-tale characters. Normally visualised as small misshapen creatures nestled in the root of a large tree, gnomes are friendly to humans and help us to restore our sense of balance with the earth when we spend some time with them.

UNLIKE GHOSTS

Elementals and devas are completely different from ghosts, who were once human. They do occupy a similar plane to ghosts, so those who can see ghosts can often see elementals as well. It is easy to confuse them. Whereas ghosts of human beings are slightly displaced souls on their way to their eventual goal, elementals are exactly where they should be, ruling nature from their own plane in their proper form.

OLD-TIME UNDERSTANDING

Ancients had a much better acquaintance with the elemental and deva kingdoms than we do. Many of what were 'pagan' fertility and harvest festivals were actually done to propitiate the elementals. The role of elementals and devas is to control the quality of the nature of their element or plant and to help form the evolution of each type of species. Humans can address them in order to learn how best employ an element in daily life. One of the few examples universally familiar to us today is the Rain Dance of the Red Indian. It is a ritual designed to ask the water elementals in clouds to produce rain. The ritual singing and dancing are done to address the elementals and persuade them to honour the request.

Many of today's traditional festivals, especially those which involve a reverence for the products of nature, emerged from the rituals designed to invoke the assistance, instruction and blessings of the elementals.

A MODERN-DAY EXAMPLE

These same principles have been used in the innovative gardens at Findhorn in northern Scotland. Begun by Peter Caddy and his wife Eileen, who as a clairvoyant was able to communicate with nature spirits, the gardens were planned according to the instructions of the devas of the garden and of each plant. In the apparently inhospitable environment of the north, the Caddys and those who joined them in their experiment, following the spirits' instructions, grew crops remarkable for their size and quantity.

TALK TO YOUR DEVA

The idea of talking to plants to make them grow has been a source of amusement for many, yet it may be the plant's deva that you're really having a conversation with. Every plant, including house plants, has its own spirit. As it is the deva which guides the way the plant grows, by chatting with it, it is possible to ask it to help the plant to be healthier, to flower or to grow in a particular shape.

MYTHIC ELEMENTALS

Fauns, sprites, pixies, and brownies all are names given in myth for members of the elemental kingdoms. The traditional forms given to these beings are similar to those reported seen by psychics today. The winged creatures, the 'Tinkerbells' of fairy tales, may be the elementals and devas as seen over the ages. And as in fairy tales, it is wise to befriend the little people, as they are often called. You never know when you might need a little fairy dust sprinkled in your life!

11

Past Lives

REINCARNATION

The concept of the soul returning again to the earth after death to begin a new life in another body appeals to some, is horrifying or shocking to others, but remains, nevertheless, a source of fascinating conjecture to almost everyone. While the belief in life after death is a common one in Western thought, reincarnation, the term for the process which actually means to return to fleshy form, remains more a source of argument and discussion. The individual soul, having lived in a series of bodies in times past, comes back to life on earth, each time with a different name, form and personality. As appealing as the idea is, not surprisingly it provokes numerous questions, of both a philosophical nature and more mechanical ones as to how such a concept actually works.

WHERE THE IDEA CAME FROM

Reincarnation is one of the tenets of Hinduism, the ancient religion of India. The Hindus believe that every soul is committed to a cycle of death and rebirth in order to learn and develop. The goal of this process is the attainment of understanding and wisdom, and the loss of attachments to this plane until eventually the soul no longer need return. In an ancient language of India, Sanskrit, a soul who has achieved this state is called *Mahatma*, Great Soul.

Gautama Buddha, the founder of the Buddhist religion, was born in India as a Hindu and brought the idea of reincarnation into the philosophy he developed. Thus reincarnation is a part of two of today's major world religions, with a geographic range stretching primarily from India to Japan.

There is some suggestion by reincarnationists of the Christian faith, as well as modern philosophical students who have researched the subject, that the concept was also a part of the Christian doctrine until about the year AD 500, when the then Pope, Origen, changed Church policy. This issue is, not surprisingly, not agreed on by church historians.

PAST-LIFE VOCABULARY

Soul or entity The individuality which enters the physical body at each incarnation, carrying traits of character, skills and abilities over from previous lives, but not necessarily those of appearance or personality.

Reincarnation The process of a soul being reborn in a series of bodies over time.

Incarnation One life for a soul.

Transmigration The process of an animal soul progressing on to a human body. The concept is believed by some in the East, but not generally accepted by reincarnationists in the rest of the world today.

Karma Energy from actions performed by or received by the soul in this or previous lives. This energy is not in itself good or bad, but represents only a potential; it can be released by action on the part of an incarnate entity in a range of ways, from

142

painful to pleasurable. The way in which it is acted out is in large part the result of awareness on the part of the entity.

Earth plane Our 'here and now', the physical world, the only place karma can be acted out.

Astral body The form the soul uses after it leaves the physical body.

Astral plane The non-physical plane of existence where the astral body resides between lives.

Guide (also angel) The being which greets souls at the end of each life to review events, lessons learned, skills gained, and to begin to plan the next incarnation.

Past-life regression The process of recalling previous lives, usually with the purpose of personal growth, understanding limitations and relationships.

GETTING A GRIP ON PAST LIVES

As intellectually interesting as the concept of reincarnation may seem, or as much as some may be intuitively attracted to it, most who have grown up in the Western world find the idea difficult to grasp, and are puzzled by its elements. It is different from the standard way of looking at life and death in the West, so that questions arise such as what happens to the soul between lives, how souls end up being who they are, and what they gain from the process of reincarnation.

The idea behind reincarnation offers an explanation for some of the conflicts and difficulties of life. But it is impossible properly to apply the philosophy to one's own life without understanding the overall picture.

WHERE DO ALL THOSE SOULS GO?

While within the community of those who believe in reincarnation there are differences of opinion, most do not think that when a soul leaves a body through death it immediately pops into a new body, but rather that it moves on the astral plane where it can review the events of the life recently completed. There are teachers who greet newly arrived souls, perhaps like the angels referred to in Christianity. Together they reflect on the life past, lessons learned, tasks left undone. The teacher then counsels and advises the soul on its next incarnation, the sex it will be (as souls have no gender), and the country and social and economic status which will most likely contribute to that particular soul's chosen path of growth. There are many influences on these choices. For example, if a soul has come from a very intellectual life, perhaps as a university professor, it might then be attracted to a rural life, possibly as a simple farmer or a shepherd. This would balance years of functioning primarily on the mental level with living a life closer to nature. There is no 'status' in life positions, merely choices based on ways in which the soul needs to grow. Therefore being rich or powerful is not an indication of a particularly accomplished soul, nor of one who has grown in wisdom beyond someone who lives in more humble circumstances. It is no more than an indication of an entity whose need to develop requires an environment of great wealth or power.

Looking at the lives of the famous, for example, the Royal Family, or members of families of great wealth, illustrates how limited in choice these lives are. The very famous cannot stroll anonymously through a park, the children of the very wealthy cannot even walk to school on their own like normal children because of fear of kidnapping. It is these limitations as well as the privileges of the life situation which shape the opportunities for the soul to learn in each life.

144

A very advanced soul may choose a quiet life in a primitive environment as many saints have done because this provides very little worldly distraction. For others a life of selfless service with little public recognition is the soul's choice for advancement.

AN OLD SOUL?

As souls repeat life after life, they gain in wisdom and spiritual qualities. While not all souls began the process of reincarnation at the same time, the starting point is not of particular importance, as each soul has the freedom to grow as rapidly as it wishes.

Early in the course of study of reincarnation, most students of the philosophy go through a phase in which they look at everyone else's life in terms of how old or evolved their soul is. The tendency is to assume that anyone who is more able, more talented, or more visibly successful than they are must be a more accomplished, or 'evolved', soul. In the West we are often seduced by worldly gain of this type. But further study usually reveals to the student that achievements of this sort are no more a sign of a soul's degree of evolution than are a noble birth or a wealthy background. It is the quieter, less immediately obvious, elements of the nature which are clearer signposts.

Old souls have not only had many, many lives, they have made use of their time in those lives well by learning and acquiring qualities which can only be gained by focus and effort. Examples are patience, wisdom, true charity and generosity, honesty, kindness. Traits of character such as these are carried over from life to life, while elements of personality are not. Thus a soul who has worked hard to be honourable will benefit from that quality for lives to come, while the gift of the gab may not make it in the translation to the next life.

SUSPICIOUSLY ATTRACTIVE

Those who are sceptical about the concept of reincarnation normally ask the same questions. The most common objection has to do with mechanics of the process. There are more people alive now than in all of previous known history. This raises the inevitable query, 'If reincarnation is true, where have all the souls of those now incarnate been until now?' The answer is that not every soul is incarnate, that is in physical form, at all times. This is the explanation given for the increasing and decreasing population (such as after the Plague of Europe) over history. During less populous times, more souls were on vacation, not embodied; now, a greater percentage are here living out lives on the physical plane.

Another question addresses the extraordinary number of claims made of previous lives as royalty or other famous historical figures such as Napoleon or Nefertiti. While most people have no memory of any past life, it seems others recall only the grand ones. While this may seem more the subject for a comedy routine, it is logical to wonder about all the reports of famous past lives and the seeming lack of ordinary ones.

WHY DON'T I REMEMBER?

The most common explanation used by reincarnationists, those who explore the theory and workings of past lives, is that since recalling what they have done every day in this life is difficult, remembering previous lives would be even more difficult. Another explanation suggests that may be of no help recalling past existences. There is a certain economy in not cluttering the mind with memories of hundreds of past lives. And as not all lives have been happy ones (which may be the reason some only remember their grand lives!) the knowledge of them would be a burden. Only when the information would advance the soul's progress is recollection encouraged. And news of previous lives may not always be easy to deal with.

A situation of this sort occurred when a woman learned of her previous life as a courtesan in the French court. She was not only told what she was, but her name as a mistress of the king. Pleased with the sound of this very glamorous and slightly naughty past, she began to study the life of her 'predecessor'. However, she discovered that the behaviour of this unsavoury character in her past had been appalling, and there was nothing of which she could be proud. She was left with a bitter taste.

Cultural conditioning is a factor in remembering as well. Everyone is more attentive to topics which interest us and are the subject of frequent conversation. Someone raised in a family keen on sport is much more likely to remember, understand and keep an eye on what's happening in the sport world. Those from a family that is more orientated to gardening will know one plant from another. But neither is likely to register an impression, no matter how strong, about previous lives, if it has not been a matter of interest and a reference point in their present life.

In countries where the idea of reincarnation is a more common one, an unusual ability in a family member, such as a musically gifted child born into a non-musical family, will be assumed to be a talent carried over from a previous life. Those who seem to have great burdens to bear in this life are equally assumed to be carrying over responsibilities not fulfilled in a previous one.

HAVEN'T WE MET BEFORE?

A persuasive aspect of reincarnation comes as an explanation for the uncanny feeling of familiarity occasionally experienced when meeting someone for the first time. There is a compelling sensation of having met before. Equally it happens when one encounters an individual to whom, for no apparent reason, you take an instant dislike.

These immediate reactions may be picking up where a

relationship left off in a previous existence. While not everyone feels the need to know the exact reason for strong responses of this sort, exploration into past lives will sometimes answer questions and help solve problems between individuals in this life. Most reincarnationists think one of the reasons for continuing rebirths is to settle all scores with others we have known in previous lives. Thus souls continue to rejoin, meeting again and again, until they reach a point of balance in relationship, with debts on neither side. Roles change to suit the purpose; a sister in one life becomes a best friend in the next. A partner from an unhappy marriage becomes a sibling, so that, by being together again, they may finally learn to live peaceably as fellow souls.

HOW THE SOUL CHOOSES

The idea then is not that the soul comes shooting into this body or that at random, like looking for a space in a car park, but rather that each life is carefully chosen to advance the development of the soul.

In the time of review between lives, the soul, with the assistance of a guide, selects the next 'course of study' for itself, and chooses the situation, family and time in history and place where it will be easiest to learn and advance the next stage of its plans. It also takes into account any obligations owed to others from previous lives and tries to arrange with those souls to be together again to take care of these matters. It is only on the earth plane that these obligations can be worked out.

The soul may have to wait a little for the best time and place with the right people around to come to pass. In the meantime, the soul will study and rest during its time on the non-physical plane.

SETTLING UP OVER LIFETIMES

Everyone has encountered someone who just can't seem to

do enough for them. Equally it has happened that one is compelled to give help to someone unknown. One explanation for situations of this sort is linked to past lives.

In the pattern of energies woven between people, the settling of debts seems to be a process which goes on over many lifetimes. Even when we are not conscious of the reason for the impulse behind doing something for another, the balance sheet gets cleared, as favours done in a previous life are returned. The obligations dealt with in this fashion are called karma.

WHAT IS KARMA?

The word *karma* comes from an ancient language of India, and of the Hindu religion, Sanskrit, and has to do with the energy produced as the result of action. In the West it is often misused in light of the Judaeo-Christian concept of paying for one's sins and evil deeds. In metaphysical circles many make the error of speaking about having 'bad karma' or 'good karma'. The term actually refers to a completely neutral force, which only balances energy; for every action there is an opposite and equal reaction. The word karma means this unacted action – left over from previous lives.

To put it simply, if you borrowed fifty pounds from a friend, but the friend died before it could be paid back, then the friend is still owed the money. Not that you meant to keep the money, but there was simply no opportunity to return it. The karmic debt will still have to be paid, but it does not mean you did anything wrong, nor would there necessarily be resistance to doing what is required to repay the debt and balance the energies. In a future life, it may not even be obvious that the reason for an act is a karmic obligation. The situation may be resolved easily, by giving the old friend a profitable tip on the races, or selling him an antique for fifty pounds under its value. There are many ways in which a balance can be regained.

The settling of karma in this way is going on constantly,

mostly unnoticed and with little drama. It is only when we resist or allow it to accumulate over many lives that these unacted actions turn into dramatic situations which might be called 'heavy karma'.

'BAD' KARMA AND 'GOOD'

There is a tendency to refer to anything unpleasant in life as a dose of 'bad karma' and anything pleasant as 'good karma', the latter clearly earned as the result of being a very virtuous person in previous lives. To say that this is simplifying the concept of karma in the extreme is an understatement.

Because karma is a neutral balancer, it is possible to equal out an obligation to another by taking that person out for a lovely meal which you both enjoy eating. You may have been the one who did the owing, but there is no reason not to enjoy the sharing. It is a pleasure to be kind to others, yet this can often be an act of equalising karma.

On occasion there may be someone who is resistant to receiving; they may end up being put in the position of being receptive in an apparently involuntary fashion. For example, they may have a flat tyre on an isolated stretch of road and the person who comes along and helps them change it not only fixes the tyre, but also takes care of a karmic obligation.

Very talented and gifted people present an interesting aspect of the action of karma. While some artists and performers have characters of great substance, there are others about whom there seems to be little to admire apart from their talent. Those interested in looking at life from the point of view of past lives wonder how it is these souls attracted such gifts – surely not because of their great qualities of character. In many cases the answer is that because their behaviour in past lives affected so many adversely, accumulating karmic debts to great numbers of people, the only way to balance it is by giving the same number of people pleasure through the use of their talents in this life. While their own character may – or may not – be developing in this life, they are releasing the bonds of their larger karmic debts.

There is great danger in judging someone else's karma based on the appearance of their life. Privileges may be proving a golden cage; deprivation may be the stimulus to growth of the soul's choice. Each carefully designs this life's gifts and challenges. In the realm of karma, all is never quite as it seems.

PAST-LIFE REGRESSION

Those interested in moving on from reading about the theory of reincarnation to exploring their own past lives, karma, relationships and what they chose to learn in this life have several options. There are three major approaches.

The first is by using intuition, self-observation. If you watch your reactions to situations and life trends, skills and, as importantly, weaknesses, a pattern will begin to be discernible. While this takes time and patience, it can reveal a great deal. A difficulty in feeling comfortable with the opposite sex could suggest previous monastic existences; a fascination with the language and culture of a particular country, happy recollections of lives there.

The second method is consulting a past-life regressionist. Some use an altered mental state or trance, from which they report to the enquirer. Others will themselves assist the enquirer to go into such a state, in order to gain access to information not normally available to the conscious mind about past lives. Techniques such as hypnosis are used, and even acupuncture is employed by some to connect with intuitive nerve meridians in the body.

The third method is to see an astrologer who is expert in past-life interpretation. This is a specialised area of astrology; it can be particularly useful in understanding psychological blocks, compulsive behaviour, problems in getting on with life, and relationships between people. All these areas are often influenced by past lives.

WHY DO I CARE ABOUT MY PAST LIVES?

Some explore past lives out of curiosity. Most often individuals first begin their study of past lives because of a personal block, a very difficult relationship or medical problem which has no apparent cause in this life.

If a relationship is not an easy one, in a family or work environment, and there is no logical explanation in this life for the problem, often an exploration of past existences will shed light on the situation. An example might be the two sisters who couldn't seem to get on. The elder, Ann, was always accusing her younger sister, Gwen, of taking her things, such as jewellery, and scarves, and losing them. The missing objects would always turn up eventually, and though Gwen protested her innocence over years, she was not believed by her parents, who assumed the younger girl was jealous of her older sister, 'borrowed' things, was not careful with them and did actually lose them. It was not until later that a friend, who had some experience as a past-life regression therapist, suggested that they see if there was an answer in past lives.

Going into a light trance, the friend immediately saw Ann and Gwen in a house, perhaps in the seventeenth century, seemingly in France. The roles were different, however, and Ann was the mistress and Gwen her maidservant. She was jealous indeed in that life and did in fact take her mistress's belongings. Ann 'remembered' the behaviour, though not the past life, and, still retaining the suspicion, she expected the person who was now her sister to continue to take her things. Though neither girl could herself recall any of the past life, the dynamic of the way they were dealing with each other rang true. They decided to try to remember that it was a new life indeed, and that Ann, in particular, need not continue to worry that her former servant would pinch her favourite scarf. As sisters, they could now share.

152

PAST-LIFE TRAP

Past lives offer a seductive excuse to those who are not willing to confront the issues of this life. As the student explores previous existences, there may be discoveries of information about great dramas past: glamour, power, or, at the other end of the spectrum, misery. The temptation is to try to recreate the previous one in this, ignoring what this new life offers.

Familiarity with a culture and civilisation are clues to a past-life connection with a particular country or region of the world. Often those who try to benefit from that by returning to the same land today are given a shock. Not only will the country have changed, as, to state the obvious, past lives do take place in the past, but the soul has changed as well. Rarely will return visits to lands of previous acquaintance yield other than memories and a sentimental journey.

Those who use their past lives as excuses are equally living out of sync with their soul's intentions. Sometimes souls swing from one extreme to another from life to life, taking the entity from wealth to poverty and from power to slavery. Though memories of the qualities of a former existence may linger, efforts to duplicate them in this life will only create conflict.

While a couple may meet and feel they have known each other in a previous life, this does not mean they must be together in this, and though it may be discovered that one was a dancer in a former incarnation, that does not mean that one should not become an accountant in this. It is true that great genius accumulates over lifetimes of focused development of a skill, so some souls do work at the same activity for many consecutive lives. But for most the pattern of incarnations is designed to keep them moving on to new experiences. While knowledge about lives past may be informative, the most important thing to remember is that the only place karma gets taken care of is in this one.

THE UNHEALED WOUND

A vigorous and active man, Brad was an expert sportsman. Good at anything physical, he could ride, ski and trek fearlessly. It was a great surprise to him when one day he was jumping a horse over a fence at a friend's new farm and was thrown, sustaining a badly dislocated shoulder and a deep wound from striking a post. In hospital his shoulder was put back in place and his wound was treated. He returned home after a few days expecting to resume his usual schedule. However, the wound would not heal and the shoulder continued to pain him so much he curtailed much of his sport. He had physiotherapy and did his best to exercise, but the pain persisted in a diabolical manner.

Again, it was a friend familiar with past lives who suggested that a regression might help. Normally dismissive of what he considered to be rubbish, Brad was now ready to try anything. The friend put him into a light trance, having him breathe deeply and visualise himself floating out of his body. Fortunately Brad was an excellent subject and quickly went 'under'. He was then told that nothing he saw or felt would endanger him, and he would recall incidents only if so directed. This is always done to protect the individual being regressed, in case a very traumatic point in a previous life is met.

Brad was told to go to the life related to his injury. He described what was clearly the same place where he had been thrown from the horse, although the countryside was different. It seemed to be England of some years ago. He was wearing a German soldier's uniform, near what appeared to be his crashed plane. He was in pain and angry for having failed in his mission. In that unforgiving frame of mind, Brad, as the soldier, died from his injuries.

When he returned to the spot where he died, in present time his friend's farm, the strong emotions from the traumatic event took over, throwing him into a state of confusion, off his horse and into the same pain that he had not released from the previous life. Instructed by the regressionist to address himself as the fallen flyer, forgiving himself and acknowledging he had done his best, Brad experienced a sudden burst of pain in the area of the wound and wept. The therapist brought him slowly back to this body and time. Shaken by the experience, he said little. But the wound healed and his shoulder is like new now.

Cases of this sort, where stubborn injuries or psychological complexes seem to resist normal treatment but yield to past-life therapy, are frequent enough to be impressive. It seems the recognition and release of the energy pent up from the previous existence allows resolution in this life. Practitioners who use these methods often take the view that whether or not these are actual experiences which happened in past lives, or merely images of events which contributed to a block in this one, results are obtained, and patients returned to full function, so they continue to employ the technique.

DIFFICULT TO PROVE

Because the concept of reincarnation goes beyond not only the physical plane, but also beyond time, it is difficult to prove. Though there are scientific enquiries now being done, some of which actually involve going to the locations of alleged previous lives to search for historical documentation of facts remembered by subjects in past-life recall sessions, there is little research acceptable to sceptics on the subject.

For those to whom reincarnation appeals because it makes the wide range of life conditions more reasonable, it is not necessary to have proof for the idea to be of philosophical comfort. And for those who have used past-life recall as a therapeutic tool, and especially if they have benefited from its use, there may be no question that the concept is a valid one. Some therapists who use past lives and reincarnation approach it as if a story were being told about the subject's previous life, eliminating the need for 'proof' or historical accuracy. They use the idea as a tool, and are, indeed, very happy with its effectiveness.

THE FINAL PROOF

If reincarnationists are correct, then they will have the last laugh. Of all the metaphysical realms, they can be certain, if their realm exists, that we each will eventually visit it. Until that time, you may find exploring your own past lives a worthwhile addition to your travels in the land of the sixth sense.

12

Palmistry and Reading the Body

Is the future written in the palm of your hand? And is it further outlined in the shape of your eyebrows, the bumps on your head, and the moles on your face?

Palm reading is often relegated in the minds of many to 'gypsies' at church fêtes. Even those who go to an astrologer for an annual check-up and regularly see their psychic, may still dismiss the idea of palm reading as ridiculous.

Yet those who employ this method think the body itself acts as a giant mirror of what we are, what we have come from and are becoming. Even those unfamiliar with palmistry technique are aware that the lines on the hand can be used in some way to reveal the fortune. But the thought of reading the bumps on the head or the moles on the face may appear pretty peculiar. Yet bizarre as it seems, each of these fields has been developed into a very precise system of investigating the character, personality and health of an individual.

READING THE BODY

The concept behind all these methods of reading the body is that there are two sources of our 'destiny' – our physical background, that is what our parents gave to us through our heredity, and what we have done with that since.

Outside of palmistry, the concept of reading the body

is not common in the Western world today. You may be more familiar with getting information about your future from some sort of external device such as an astrological horoscope or Tarot cards, or from a psychic, but the body has been used for auguries over the ages. Physiognomy, the term used to describe reading the body, is one of the most ancient systems for the study of the character, personality and destiny of a person. It is likely to have been in use long before astrology was employed for this purpose.

Certainly there are writings still used today in the Chinese form of physiognomy which date from as early as 2000 BC. They study the shape of the whole body, describing it in terms of animals and crediting those forms with certain traits and potentials. According to this system, it is possible to be one of many birds from phoenix to duck, or perhaps a tiger or an elephant (which is more desirable than you might think, as an elephant person is respected and rich). Further parts of the body such as ears, noses, and eyebrows were classified as refinements of indications of character and of the likelihood of happiness and success.

As much as it has been a part of life in the Orient, physiognomy never really got a grip in the West until the last century. Then it flourished as part of the passion of that time for systematic investigation and classification of the physical world. The idea that by comparing and analysing various parts of the body a pattern would be revealed made sense to the nineteenth-century mind. It was considered that everyone had a head, hands, and feet which were all basically similar in structure, yet no two were identical, and so the differences, if studied, could yield a wealth of information. Even today this is true, with fingerprints; the prints on every finger of every person are unique so that one found at the scene of a crime is considered adequate proof that the individual whose print matches was present.

Physiognomy Study of the shape of the body and the structures of its parts in order to reveal information about the whole.

Phrenology Classification of the bumps of the head as a key to the character of an individual.

Palmistry Belief that the form of the hand, its shape, texture, as well as the palm itself reveal both character and destiny; later divided up to include the following:

    Chirognomy The study of the shape of the hand alone which reveals the strengths and weaknesses of the character.

    Chiromancy The analysis of the lines of the palm to tell the events and future.

Podoscopy Reading of the feet to reveal the character.

Molosophy Analysis of the location of the moles on the body to indicate character and potential events.

(I) READING THE HAND

PALMIER DAYS

The granddaddy of physiognomical techniques, palm reading, goes back to at least 3000 BC in ancient India and China. It is still extremely common in India, as it is in the Middle East. The reading of the palm concentrates on two aspects – the structure, shape, colour and texture of the hand, which reveal the character of the individual, and the actual lines of the palm which reveal the events of the past and future.

Today in the West, especially amongst those who prefer to emphasise the free-will aspect of their nature, palmistry, understandably, has fallen out of favour. The shape and size of the hand is fixed, as, you might assume, would be the lines on the palm. Many dismiss this area of the metaphysical without exploring it, because there is a feeling that if the future is written in the palm of your hand, then equally it would seem that you're stuck with it. And who wants to hear about that?

In India not only do professionals read palms, but there are many knowledgeable amateurs who have studied for years and will look at palms. It is common to see friends peering into palms and interpreting them at social gatherings. They will monitor each other's palms and watch as old lines change and new lines appear. Which, over the years, they do. While the shape of your hand is not going to change unless you gain or lose a great deal of weight, the lines of the palm actually do change as you do.

IS THE FUTURE IN THE PALM OF YOUR HAND?

The question remains: how precisely can anyone tell about the future from the palm of the hand? The study of palmistry is confusing to the beginner because not only are the lines themselves difficult to discern, but there are several systems in which the same lines mean quite different things. If you wanted to learn palmistry yourself, it would take years to be able to do it well. It is not simple and only the experience of looking at and comparing many palms and seeing what happens to the people attached to them will give a deeper understanding of it.

Experts consider that the hand and the palm, with their distinctive and individual shape and lines, expose our inner nature. It is true that the lines on the palm do change, and often dramatically, over time. Those who are knowledgeable enough to look at their own have seen shifts in the lines within months of a major life decision having been made.

In addition to the obvious traits of character being revealed by the palm, an experienced reader should be able to give information on the emotional nature, capacity for relationships, and the timing; abilities and talents and potential for success; health and illness; money and how you handle it; travel; and even luck.

As always in the realm of metaphysics, when actually going for a consultation, it will be necessary to decide whether to see a reader who is destiny-orientated or one who encourages the use of free will to alter the indications on the palm which you may not like. Some readers will encourage you to take the future — into your own hands!

CHARACTER AND FUTURE

All palm-reading systems are divided into two parts: the study of the shape and size of the hand which has to do with character, and of the lines on the palm itself which reveal the events past and future, the real 'fortune'.

In most readings quite a time will be spent looking at the *back* of the hands, the texture, the shape of the fingers and of the nails. Some of the conclusions which the palmist draws are the obvious ones. A smooth-skinned hand with tapering nails indicates a delicate, perhaps not overly practical person, while a rough hand with square nails probably belongs to a sensible sort. Remembering that palmistry evolved from observation, it is easy to see its origins from looking only at the backs of hands.

The way in which the fingers are held in relation to each other is studied. Each finger is named after a planet and an aspect of character; ones held away from the others do not mix so easily with the energies represented by the others. The shape, length relative to each other, and straightness of each finger is noted. Though perhaps not pretty, be grateful for knotty knuckles, a sign of practicality. The palmist will look to see if light is visible between the fingers at the base of the palm. If so, this is the space through which money is said to run out.

The palmist takes the hand and gently bends the fingers back to test the flexibility of mind. The set and size of the thumb will be considered. The lower set thumb is considered to have greater agility of mind. This is a logical conclusion as it is indeed the thumb which is used as a 'tool' finger in handling objects. A thumb placed lower on the hand has a better gripping angle than one more highly placed. (In India, the home of a great number of serious palmists, there are those who specialise in the reading of the thumb alone, considering it adequate to tell the entire tale of the character: thumbology.) The reader focuses on the character aspect first, so that when the time comes to look at the events in the palm, they can judge what your response will be to life changes.

THE MOUNTING TALE

The palmist will now look directly at the palms. It's not time for the fortune yet. The mounts of the palms will next be inspected. These are the soft fleshy pads at the base of the thumb, along the outside of the hand, and in the small areas at the base of and at the tip of each finger. Each of these is called by the name of a planet and is associated with a planet's character, because of the close association of palmistry and astrology in India, where most of the palmistry techniques we now use come from.

The easiest of the mounts to recognise is the mount of Venus. At the base of the thumb and enclosed by one of the curving lines, this mount has to do with love, appreciation of beauty and sensuality. As with all good things, so with mounts such as this one, more is not necessarily better. As you can imagine, too much unrestrained appreciation of these things could make a plump romantic indeed. The ideal mount is full but not overly fleshy.

The reader will inspect each of these mounts and describe its power. Subtle variations in their size and placement not discernible by the untrained will be commented on and analysed. In addition to the Mount of Venus, there are mounts of Jupiter, Saturn, Sun or Apollo, Jupiter, Mercury (under each of the fingers), two for Mars, on opposite sides of the palm, and the Moon.

THE LINE-UP OF LINES

Finally it will be time to turn to the lines of the palm, and begin to explore the tale of life's events. But first it must be determined which hand is dominant. If you look closely at the lines in the hands, you can see they are actually different. The 'dominant' hand reflects what has been made of one's destiny since birth, the other still mirrors that original destiny. Most palmists consider the hand with which you write to be the dominant hand. There are a few who feel the left hand is the dominant hand for women and the right for men. Go along with whatever approach your palmist uses. Though there are some rules, palmistry is a very personal and subjective kind of analysis and each reader will have their own way of reading.

The reading of the lines must be done in bright light; palmists look at subtle lines in the palm and need good light to see them. Some palmists prefer to work from a palm print for this reason. Made by covering the entire palm with ink and pressing it on paper, it is a messy process, but properly done will reveal all of the most delicate lines and allow more concentrated study.

The palmist who works directly with the hand will slightly relax your palm; a tautly stretched palm will not show the lines as well. The lines are judged by their clarity, whether they are deep and run straight or broken or chained as they progress across the palm. The uninitiated will probably have difficulty even seeing many of the lines the palmist is looking at, so don't worry if you can't see what's clear, what's chained and what's not.

There are three major lines which will probably be the first to be analysed. Most people have all three. The life line runs in a crescent shape along the base of the thumb, dividing the rest of the palm from the Mount of Venus, which you may have already recognised. The other two run across the palm, more or less parallel, in the upper half of the palm under the fingers. These two are called the head line and the heart line.

These will be analysed to gain a picture of the timing and intensity of events in your life. The life line chronicles events in years from its inception between the thumb and first finger as it curves toward the bottom of the palm. All the other lines, even the much less visible ones, can be timed in a similar manner, each revealing matters from the realm it rules. There are lines of fate, or destiny, health, and ones for money, intuition, spirituality, marriage, children and the like.

STARS IN YOUR PALM?

The palmist will now begin to look at the assortment of cross hatchings in the palm which to the experienced eye are discernible as the shapes of stars, crosses, squares, triangles and grills. These formations, which can appear on any part of the palm, will be clues as to the further refinement of the reading. For example, the Mount of Venus may not be very large, which would suggest a not particularly loving or sensual nature, but with the presence of a star in the centre of that mount, the likelihood of having warm relationships is considerably improved.

There are tiny little lines at the edge of the palm which are of great interest to all – the marriage lines. These are small lines on the outer edge of the palm under the little finger. In an age where major relationships do not always result in marriage, the traditional interpretation of these lines is being revised. But still the number of lines there are still does indicate the number of major relationships in the life.

WHEN YOU GO

The best source for a good palm reader is a referral by a friend. Magazine classified columns and metaphysical centres will often have listings of readers. If selecting from a source such as this, then ask how the reader learned palmistry and how long he or she has been doing it. Don't be embarrassed to ask. If someone is just beginning it will be important to know that in order to be able to evaluate the reading. It is also worthwhile to enquire the background tradition of the type of reading being done. There are differing cultural values which you will want to be aware of.

Fees for palm reading will range widely. For those who are full-time consultants with many years experience, expect to pay a bit more than for those who work at it part-time or as a hobby. It is rare that the charges are high; palmistry can be very good value for money!

Two of the cultures which have a strong tradition of palm reading are the Indian and the gypsy. Each has many fine readers who both understand the art and are good at expressing their knowledge.

While the palm-reading techniques of Indians are excellent, in a reading it is vital to look out for cultural confusion. Ancient traditions of interpretation assume, for example, that marriage and having a large number of children is the goal of every woman. Though this is not even the case in India itself any more, many palmists will make this assumption when interpreting the palm. Recently a woman who writes for a living was told by an Indian palmist she would marry very soon and stop writing. While pleased about the idea of marriage, she likes her work and was distressed to think she would stop. But by traditional Indian palmistry marriage has precedent in a woman's palm over other indications. Unless she had asked for clarification, she would have gone away worried that if she got one thing she wanted, she would lose another.

As always, ask to tape the reading. Palmistry often includes information which reaches far into the future, and a tape is the most reliable reference, even if it is later transcribed. Go prepared with questions. A palmist is not a psychic, so exact timing of events to the month and week is not likely, nor are descriptions of others in your life. Do expect to hear about turning points and new directions long before they become part of your conscious awareness.

Remember, the lines of the palm, from which the future is read, are the result of the way the hands are used in the most literal sense. It is not a great leap to see how these lines might mirror the way energies are used. As always the direction of things can be altered by directing energy otherwise. This combination, the knowledge of the potential pictured in the palm of your hand and the willingness to refocus your aims will allow you to truly say that your own future is in the palm of your hand.

(II) READING THE BODY

While it is likely that at sometime you will have your palm read, even if it is only at a church fête, you are not as likely to come across the following two types of methods of reading. Yet they are so fascinating that you might enjoy finding out about them.

CHINESE PHYSIOGNOMY

Re-orientating yourself

The palm reading about which you have just learned, and with which most of the Western world is familiar, is a descendant of this ancient system of body study. Chinese physiognomy focuses on the shape of the whole body, interpreting the meaning of its shape, as well as the form of parts of it. This system detailed the potential of the individual for contribution to the community as well as for personal wellbeing. In traditional Chinese physiognomy only men were read, as it was considered that a woman's destiny was linked with that of the men in her life, a concept which would perhaps not be as well accepted today.

The Chinese see the world as having five elements: earth, wood, fire, metal, and water. Every body, as well as every part of that body, is of one or a combination of these types. While no shape is superior to another, some of them combine more happily with others; for example, someone who is a pure water shape would be round of form and wise and wealthy. But if the earth element were added, it would bring ill-health and bad luck throughout life!

As with most very old systems, the Chinese is rather absolute in its interpretations, though it also taught that even the most dire-seeming indications can be changed by character and kindness on the part of the individual.

The Five Body Shapes

Water Round but not fat body, so that the bones are not visible. Hands soft with tapering fingers. Nature is calm, quiet and direct.

Earth Large features, big nose, mouth, strong bones and muscles, even a loud voice. Hands large and fleshy. True and faithful, will be rich and live a long time.

Fire Long head, wide chin and domed forehead. Dry and rough colouring and voice. Hands bony and sharp with sinews showing. Polite and disciplined but temperamental, so fortunes may rise and fall.

Wood Tall, thin and strong with bones showing, especially in hands, which are very knotted looking. Kind with wealth coming late in a long life.

Metal Square with solid strong muscles, balanced facial features. Very square hands and nails. Works hard, does not play easily, responsible, prefers life in an ordered world such as the military.

These are the five elements and examples of the types of energies they represent. If you don't see yourself exactly in one of them, it may be because you are a blend of two.

Chinese Zoo

It probably takes a practised eye to tell the difference between a duck-shaped person and a mandarin-duck-shaped one, but the difference is important because while a duck has good friends and a strong stomach, a mandarin duck likes to flirt and uses bad language. There is a wide variety of animal shapes, and each is viewed as giving very specific characteristics from poverty to wealth, greed to generosity. Happier animals are the crane, magpie, tortoise, lion, camel, rabbit and horse. You would not be so lucky if you were a pig, partridge, mountain tiger, or crow.

The Five Long and The Five Short

Also of importance in taking a general analysis is the combination of five parts of the body; the head, face, arms, hands, and legs. If you have 'The Five Long', all these elements of your body will be proportionately long and balanced. You must also have a bright complexion and cheery character to go with them. Otherwise you will gain no advantage from 'The Five Long'.

If you have 'The Five Short' you must also have small bones. It is even more important that someone with 'The Five Short' has balanced facial features for a good reading.

Feature Selection

In order to draw a conclusion, Chinese physiognomy blends many details. The shape of the body, both looking at the element it is, as well as the animal shape. In addition the facial features are considered, of which there are five, and the overall face shape, which is then itself divided into thirteen parts for analysis!

The Chinese Features

Eyebrows There are over thirty types of brows, catalogued by shape, length, quantity and direction of growth of hair. Details such as these reveal those with bushy brows which grow upward will be temperamental and are likely to have guilt in their old age because of their previous actions in their youth. Widely set eyebrows suggest that you have a forgiving nature but are forgetful, while a mole

there indicates a good family background and education.
Eyes As this system was developed in China, where the eyes are normally brown, eye colour is not mentioned. There is great analysis not only of the eye shape, but also of the relationship between the brow and the eye. Low brows are generally not viewed favourably. Large eyes show drive and a liking for the opposite sex. Even wrinkles around the eyes are analysed and are a good sign but only if they run upwards. Attractive but watery looking eyes belong to someone with a lustful nature.

Nose The nose is always studied in combination with the cheekbones. Cheekbones which are more pronounced than the nose are not a good sign, as the nose is considered the commander of the face. A good, larger rather than smaller nose is a happy augury; it will hopefully also be straight and not upturned. A woman's nose reveals her marriage partner: if it is strong, not too thin and the nose bone does not show then she can expect a fine husband.

Mouth The corners of the mouth are especially important to the Chinese, as is its fullness. Ideally, the corners will turn up, a sign of kindness. Lips will be full, not tightly pursed which indicates meanness. An upper lip which covers the lower one is the ideal for the Chinese male, as it indicates he will be a good provider.

Ear The ear is important in reading because it does not move and therefore cannot be deceptive. Ideally it should be large and close to the head with the outer edge being smooth and rounded. It should line up with the eyebrow and the tip of the nose, too high and the bearer's friends will find him to be an exhibitionist, too low and the intellect is in question.

Facing the Face Facts

When viewing the entire face, Chinese physiognomists divide it for study in a number of different ways. The Thirteen Positions refer to the division of the face horizontally from top to bottom.

The lines on the forehead between the eyebrows are studied for indications of success and wealth. A Y-shaped line suggests that a wealthy person will help you; two lines signal a difficult life; and a third an anxious disposition. If the lines cross, you may have hobbies which are criminal! The indentation in the space between the nose and the upper lip gives information about children; narrow at the top and wide at the bottom gives many healthy offspring, if it is narrow and shallow not only will there be few children, you are also bad-tempered yourself.

Twelve points on the face further refine the reading. The area of the temples, cheekbones, eyelids and below the eyes, tip of the nose, and chin all contribute to the information not only about the future, but also the timing. For example a mole on the nose is lucky, but a scar in the same spot warns of trouble around the age of forty-four.

The face itself is also viewed as a progression of time. The top third, the forehead, reveals the background and childhood, the centre portion the middle years and the bottom part the old age. This is one time a double chin is a good sign. It indicates many wives and a happy old age.

Chinese Palmistry

The palm is only one of the many tools used in Chinese reading. It is considered to be a deciding factor if the other information is not conclusive because lines on the hand take longer to form and last longer. The left hand of a man and the right hand of a woman are considered the dominant hand; the other shows the heritage of family and background.

Since the Chinese system of physiognomy is thought to be the parent of modern palmistry, it is no surprise that the lines and their meaning are very similar to those in use in West today. The life, head and heart lines are allocated in the same manner and timing calculated in the same direction. Even the marriage lines are located on the outer edge of the palm.

PHRENOLOGY

Getting Ahead

Phrenology is the art of reading the bumps on the head to know the character. It was very much in fashion in the nineteenth century; it is equally out of favour now. Its basic concept is that the skull, which is really what is read, holds the brain, so that undulations in the bone of the skull would pass on and influence function of the brain. Different portions of the skull were associated with various aspects of character and personality.

First studied and organised early in the 1800s by the German Dr Gall, phrenology was picked up by a Scot called George Combe, who popularised it in England. He divided the bumps on the skull into four groups: fundamental qualities of character; feelings; perception; and reason and knowledge. This is only the basic breakdown and Combe listed thirty-seven bumps to be felt and analysed. Feel your own head and imagine trying to discern thirty-seven individual areas of undulation. This makes finding little lines on the palm seem simple and may be why phrenology has not become a popular hobby – it's too difficult.

Here's a sampling of bump interpretations:

Bridge of the nose If well developed you understand *shape* and form such as geometric concepts; is also strong in sculptors. If under-developed, trouble with spatial concepts and may tend to run into things.

Centre back base of the skull when prominent suggests strong *sexuality*; too large, an obsession with sex.

Just over and in front of the ear reveals the *appetite*. Under-developed will not enjoy food or other pleasures, overly present could be a compulsive eater.

Under the eye signals *verbal expression*. A flat area here gives the silent type; fully developed means a speaker, writer and possibly an argumentative person.

MOLEOSOPHY

Spots Before Your Eyes

Very popular as a device for reading in Victorian England, moles are still considered today in readings in India. Is it any stranger to rely on darkly pigmented spots on your body to reveal your character than the shape of your hand? Judge for yourself.

Location of Moles and Their Meanings

Forehead Right: intelligence and wealth. Left: extravagance.
Eye (outer corner) Thrift.
Eyebrow Right: happy marriage. Left: not as easy a marriage.
Ear Reckless, gossipy, jealous; but all can be overcome.
Nose Travel, propriety.
Lip Pleasure loving, sensual.
Jaw Success in business, admired and respected for ethics.
Throat Can be accident prone, but able and successful.
Shoulder Difficult times.
Breast Right: well married and content. Left: seductive, possibly too much so. Centre: adequate money, unexciting life.
Stomach Can be selfish and greedy.
Hips Strong and healthy children.
Thighs Right: warm temperament, happy life. Left: good-natured, though with loss, poverty.
Ankle Fashionable and active life.
Foot Right: love of travel. Left: bright mind.

YOUR OWN BODY OF KNOWLEDGE

Now you've completed your conducted tour of the body as a key to character and destiny. It may be shocking to think that, though you were raised 'not to judge a book by its cover', you now know how to judge individuals by the way they look as well as tell their fortune. The

American president Abraham Lincoln was once reproached for commenting that he did not trust a particular man because he didn't like the man's looks. Lincoln replied he considered anyone who did not judge others by their looks was a fool. Perhaps he had studied physiognomy in a previous life.

13

Numerology

With the ever-increasing presence of maths and sciences, it seems that a system which uses numbers to analyse character and destiny must surely be a product of today's computer era. Its clean, sleek scientific precision goes with the idea of computers. But, as space age as it appears, numerology, surprisingly, dates back a long way, all the way to Ancient Greece.

The concept of numerology is that every person, every date, and even ideas have an essential vibration which can be expressed by numbers; and each of those numbers has a special significance which can be interpreted. Thus the date of your birth, your name, even your address, could be reduced by numerological calculation to a single number which carries a particular energy, traits and potential. Everyone has a personal number. Numerologists also analyse historical events and study the character of each year by the use of universal numbers, which reveal the focal energy behind each year, month and day. These universal numbers can be combined with your own personal numbers to see how events might affect your life.

THE GREEK KEY TO NUMBERS

Pythagoras, the founder of numerology, was born on the Greek island of Samos in the sixth century BC. All too well known to every geometry student, Pythagoras was actually a philosopher. He believed it was possible to bring order and understanding to the chaotic universe by using numbers as symbols. With his system of numbers he believed that everything, ideas, objects and sounds, could be identified and organised. He thought history could also be analysed numerologically, and he divided it up into cycles to which he gave numerical values.

One story of the way he came to discover this theory is that while passing by a blacksmith's shop, he heard the sounds of four different smith's hammers making four harmonic tones. He had the four anvils weighed and their proportions were discovered to be in increments of 6, 8, 9 and 12. It was from this discovery that he developed the theory there was a numerical harmonic among all things in the universe.

Pythagoras not only used his knowledge in mathematics, but in music, and healing arts and rituals, teaching these to his students at his secret society located in Crotona, in southern Italy.

CABALA'S HIDDEN WISDOM

The *Cabala* (spelled in a variety of ways, including *Kabbala*) is a book of Jewish mysticism. Actually meaning 'hidden wisdom' in Hebrew, the language of the Jewish religion, it was passed along by oral tradition for centuries before it was written down in book form. Composed of a number of different teachings, the texts appear to have been compiled in the years from about AD 200 to 1200. It emphasises the enigma of the universe and of the nature of God, meditating on the paradox of good and evil in the diversity of the human situation.

As part of that meditation there is a specific study of numbers called 'gematria'. In Hebrew letters have always stood as symbols on their own as well as being the building blocks of words. In gematria, the significance between those letters and numbers is explored. Study of *Cabala* includes the study of the numerical frequency of letters in a search for hidden meaning in interpreting scripture.

EVERYTHING HAS A NUMBER

Modern numerologists believe, just as Pythagoras did, that the world and everyone in it can be ordered, analysed and studied by reduction to a single number. The primary numbers are the single digits from one to nine. Usually the numbers eleven, twenty-two and thirty-three, which are referred to as master numbers are included. Each number has a character of its own. Over the centuries many numerologists have also been astrologers, so each number has acquired a planet as well which represents its energy.

The most frequently analysed elements are an individual's birth date and name. Calculations are quite simple; the numbers of the date are added together and reduced to the primary number. In finding the number for the name, the letters are first reduced to numbers by a method in which the letter A corresponds to the number one; B, two; C, three; and so on. The numbers are then added up until finally the single digit primary number is reached. Obviously, using numerology is no time to fudge on birth dates. Making yourself younger could entirely change your destiny! Equally, the entire name must be reported as given at birth, including all the middle names. If a different name or married name is used, that will also be considered, but in numerology it is what you started out with that matters.

HOW TO GET YOUR NUMBER

The method behind numerological calculations is very straightforward indeed. Everything is reduced to a primary number, and each primary number has a meaning. The process of numerical reduction is not difficult to understand.

For dates, the day, month and year are listed in numerical form. For example, 22 December 1954 becomes 22/12/1954. These numbers are added as individual units as follows:

22 $(2+2=4)$	becomes 4
12 $(1+2=3)$	becomes 3
1954 $(1+9+5+4=19)$	becomes 19

Any numbers that are not single digits are further reduced, so the 19 is added thus:

$(1+9=10)$ becomes 10 and the nought is dropped.

This results in a series of numbers which are then again added

$$4+3+1=8$$

Eight is the numerological value for 22 December 1954. If that is your birth date, that becomes your destiny number, or life path number. If it is the day a company was started, or the date of a wedding, it is equally the destiny number of that event. The same process is used for any date.

In numerological analysis, the destiny number is viewed as revealing the fundamental nature. Explained at greater length below, the elements the destiny number describes are inborn traits and cannot be changed any more than you can change the colour of your eyes. Your destiny means the direction and pace at which you function, the sort of life which you would find fulfilling. Numerologists believe that the goal is to develop strengths of character within the range of possibilities of your number.

But this is not the only number necessary for a numerological analysis.

IT IS ALL IN A NAME

A numerologist will analyse your name as well. This is called the expression number. It concerns the side the world sees. Just as when first meeting people you tell them your name, not your birth date, so the expression number describes the part of you which is shared with others: the personality, work, the way of thinking. And, just as your name can be changed, the way your expression number is used can be altered more easily than can the destiny number.

The procedure for calculating the expression number is slightly more complicated than the destiny number as the letters of the name must first be turned into numbers before they can be added up. This is done in a simple process using a chart in which the letters correspond to numbers.

1	2	3	4	5	6	7	8	9
A	B	C	D	E	F	G	H	I
J	K	L	M	N	O	P	Q	R
S	T	U	V	W	X	Y	Z	

The numerologist first takes the name at birth. Remember this one time to reveal your full name, otherwise the number derived won't be the real you at all.

For Anne Louise Kyrke the numerical value would be calculated in this manner.

$$\begin{array}{ccc}
\text{A N N E} & \text{L O U I S E} & \text{K Y R K E} \\
1\ 5\ 5\ 5 & 3\ 6\ 3\ 9\ 1\ 5 & 2\ 7\ 9\ 2\ 5 \\
1+5+5+5 & 3+6+3+9+1+5 & 2+7+9+2+5 \\
=16 & =27 & =25 \\
1+6=7 & 2+7=9 & 2+5=7
\end{array}$$

$$7+9+7=23$$
$$2+3=5$$

The expression number of Anne Louise Kyrke is five. If Anne Louise gets married or becomes an actress and changes her name, her expression number will remain five, but the numbers of the new name will be added in the same manner and that name's impact will be considered in the interpretation.

THE MEANING OF THE NUMBERS

The nine primary numbers, plus the three master numbers, eleven, twenty-two, and thirty-three, can be used for an interpretation of a personal numerological chart. The same numbers are used for calculating and interpreting dates. The substance of the meaning is the same no matter what is being analysed. For example, whether it is a person or a year, one is the number which is always at the beginning, at the forefront of what's happening.

The destiny (birth date) or expression (name) numbers are interpreted separately. Each of the two is then compared to have a full understanding of the individual nature.

One
The Sun

Not the ideal cog in a wheel, One is all about breaking loose and starting anew. One years are the beginnings of new cycles. One people love starting up things as well. Loathing repetition, endowed with limitless energy, an original in every way, One people are not easy to get to conform. Used properly, One is the energy behind new inventions. One people are the leaders, inspirers of others. Allowed to turn inward, One energy becomes self-indulgent and self-centred, unreasonable and easily angered.

Two
The Moon

Kind, preferring an ordered existence, Two is ever seeking balance and makes a personal effort to contribute to that state in the world. Two years are a time of restoring balance, Two energy is everywhere calming. Not needing to make a splash, Twos are quiet additions to any environment. Sensitive and artistic themselves, Twos must be careful not to be too tolerant of others who could well take advantage of their good nature.

Three
Venus

Cheering, joyous, creative, Three is entertaining and lovable. A Three year is a time of warm social encounters and events, and neither the year nor the person can be expected to be attentive to details. Wide ranging in acquaintance, Threes are family orientated as well, loving to bring people together and see them happy. All that fun can mean that not much ever gets done in life, and Three must watch out for wasting time.

Four
Saturn

Earthy, square as the number implies, four is the energy behind concrete achievement. A Four year is a time of diligence, a Four's life one of considered application of effort. More satisfied with a sense of accomplishment than one of merriment, Fours must learn to relax; being out in nature is the most restful activity for Fours, so getting them to stop and smell the flowers is a wonderful idea.

Five
Mars

Exploration, experimentation, expansion; Five can't wait to get out of wherever it is. An energy of change and movement, as a year, Five will herald the introduction of new trends. Five people must have the new in their lives regularly, needing to just pick up and go, see a different part of the world. Not for Fives are yearly time-shares in holiday villas! If not in a position to have the change they need, Fives will whine and be miserable company for others.

Six
Jupiter

Fundamentally happy and balanced, the only number divisible by both odd (three) and even (two) numbers, Six has an intuitive sense of appropriateness. In Six years it seems everyone realises we all have to live on one planet together and make an effort to make it a more pleasant experience. In the same way, Sixes add in their own way to the world, often achieving a great deal without much apparent effort because the primary goal is more orientated to others' welfare. So good natured are Sixes that even the dark side is one of concern – the tendency to brood over the welfare of others.

Seven
Mercury

Analysis, everything reduced to a mental list, Sevens just can't stop thinking. Lifted to its highest potential, Seven can inspire others with ideas, at its lowest it can be the energy of narrow-minded dogma. The essence of the ivory-tower intellectual, a Seven is happiest when work requires thought; law, teaching, accountancy. A Seven year is as quiet as a Seven prefers life to be, no upsets, rather a refined progression of interesting events. Stuck in a rut, Sevens can be oblivious to the feelings of others and need to change their life and work pattern every so often to avoid this.

Eight
Sun

Action and achievement are the obsessions of Eight. Nothing is done by halves and failure is intolerable to an Eight. With the energy of the self-made entrepreneur, Eight lives all of life at full speed. As an Eight is a whirlwind to be around, equally an Eight year will bring action and results in the world. Miserable when not out conquering new worlds, Eights can be relentless to those around them. They need to learn that balance in life means being able to slow down enough to enjoy life's successes.

Nine
Mars or All The Planets

All things to all people, Nines complete the cycle of the primary numbers by having something to contribute to everyone. While ambitious in the sense of seeking new goals and enjoying the process of achieving them, Nines constantly see the broader spectrum and will be happiest in work which will allow the interest in others and need for changing horizons to be satisfied. A Nine year involves finishing up all the projects of the previous cycle. A Nine must watch out lest there be too many projects which dilute and scatter the energies.

In addition to the preceding primary numbers, the three master numbers, eleven, twenty-two and thirty-three, are considered if they appear, even though they too are reduced into the primary number. For example, someone born 10 February 1952 ($10/2/1952 = 11 = 1 + 1 = 2$) would be both an eleven and a two, as eleven both stands on its own and is reduced to two.

Master numbers are considered to be signals of great power, vision, and possible spiritual achievement.

Eleven
Neptune

Visionary, Elevens go around with their fairy wand, touching other people's lives. They may appear to be working at a job, or at being a home maker, but they hold the energy of transformation. Whether quietly inspired or openly a teacher, the spiritual element is always present in an Eleven's life. An Eleven year is full of transition, some of it so subtle that it is only understood at a later time. Not practical, Elevens don't notice if they are being taken advantage of. They can be the vanguard of new trends. Misled, Elevens can be lured into disillusionment, bitterness and decadence.

Twenty-two
Uranus

Power. The combination of the practical and the magical, Twenty-two has a tremendous burden because anything he does has greater impact than any of the other numbers. Able to achieve in the world, Twenty-twos can also change it for the better. Often working at a level where the potential for misuse of power is great, there is temptation at every turn. The choice between beneficence and grandiosity must be made daily. The negative can be as powerful as the positive, a great responsibility. Twenty-two years are equally creative and pivotal.

Thirty-three
Pluto (?)

Trusting, idealistic, kind, Thirty-threes are, quite simply, good people. Sharing Six's quality of kindliness, these combine it with a sensitivity and compassion which can draw them to causes and give them the ability to work well in very difficult situations. Thirty-three years are the years when everyone gets on the bandwagon to fix up the world and have peace. If Thirty-threes sound saintly, they are. So gentle and with little sense of the practical, they can be misunderstood and misunderstand other less tender souls and are in danger of being overly sensitive as the result of this.

SUMMING IT UP

These are the numbers, the alphabet of numerology. These numbers and their interpretations are the basis from which all numerological readings are derived. You have learned two techniques which are the easiest to do and understand. Numerologists use a wide range of other techniques to reveal information about the timing and character of events in life and in the world.

The two methods shown for calculating the personal number of an individual are but the most basic. If you consult a numerologist the numbers will fly fast and furious across the page as the numerologist manipulates the letters of your name into projections of the future, combines your birth date with the year's number to give information about the year, and talks about your cycles.

Many numerologists are more interested in the world cycles, and believe that by using numerology to analyse the years past each of us may learn from history and perhaps not repeat it. Some are experts at this sort of analysis and will check out financial markets, business propositions and national economies using the same numbers as in personal analysis, interpreting them with a different slant.

IF YOU GO – WHO'S REALLY GOT YOUR NUMBER?

On the first visit to a numerologist most people are interested in an analysis of their own personality, what's happening in their lives and in learning about those who are close.

In discussions, your destiny or life path number (birth date) and expression number (birth name) will certainly be calculated. There are variations and extensions of these which the numerologist may employ. One includes taking the consonants and vowels from your name and adding them up separately. The number which results from the consonants is called the soul number and expresses the deepest nature, the drive behind it all. The vowels add up to the impression number, which is how you come across to others.

Other names, a married name or a special name for work, will be discussed and compared; how the new name changes or adds to your impact. Many people consult a numerologist when they are thinking of changing a name, selecting a name for a child or even for a business to find out if the name 'adds up to something'. It is often easy to tell the name of someone who has altered their name at a numerologist's suggestion. They will use an initial as part of their name, suggested to make the numbers add up to a 'better' number than before and make the name balance out.

The consultant will analyse your life as a series of figures are drawn, usually triangles, and will rapidly fill in and add up numbers listing more opportune years, months and even days. All this addition will result in the personal year number, which will reveal the year's character and what to expect and what not to hope for.

CAN YOU ESCAPE YOUR NUMBER?

Numerology has a very philosophical origin. It draws on ancient cultures which have deeply considered views of life. Some numerologists present their information couched in those philosophical terms. But it seems that many who practise numerology are very absolute in their interpretation of what the numbers of the name and date mean, especially in the predictive sense. If you don't object to being told in such absolute terms what you can hope to accomplish in, for example, the coming year, then the more destiny-orientated numerologists will be fine. But if you prefer to be able to 'negotiate' your future, and see a reading of any sort as providing guidelines, then some numerologists may present a problem.

A career woman went to consult her numerologist at a time she was planning to start a number of new ventures. She was told she was beginning a 'seven' year and she would not get anything accomplished no matter what she did. Slightly set back by this news, she, being a New Yorker and finding a good challenge stimulating, set about working on her projects and actually expanded her work and world during her 'non-productive' year.

Even with numerology, there are variations of technique. In America, the date is usually written with the month *before* the day; this changes some numerological calculations and the results, not so much with the name, but with the numbers regarding the cycles. Equally, names from different languages have different vibrations numerologically. If a name as it is used in English has had to be translated phonetically from a language with a different script, as would a name from one of the Indian languages or from Arabic, there is some question as to whether the letter values are the same. Even with numerology, then, there is some variation possible and sophisticated and experienced numerologists have developed their own opinions about this question.

Not all numerologists are quite so absolute in their views and in the way they present their interpretations to their clients. Do remember, no matter what a consultant says, you have the last word. If what has been said is too absolute and it gives the feeling of having no choice, first ask the consultant if that is what they really mean to say. And if it is, disregard anything said you do not like.

DO YOU WANT TO DO IT YOURSELF?

Basic numerology is not difficult to learn. You have already learned to calculate destiny numbers and expression numbers. It is only necessary to remember the traits of the nine primary numbers in order to begin to interpret other numbers. But be aware how easy it is to make absolute statements. With a system which is so easy to learn, it is tempting to become an instant expert. Interpretations stated in too bold a manner do no one a favour.

If you find you enjoy your explorations, there are books and classes offered to expand your knowledge.

MAKING IT COUNT

Now it is possible to check not only the numerical significance behind names and dates, but how addresses add up, the vibration of phone numbers, even that of the day you plan to begin your holiday. Pythagoras, who started it all, believed everything in the universe had a numerological value. Now you can analyse yourself and those around you, checking out your numbers and those of your family. You can use numerology to see how your world adds up.

14

Healing

Healer. The word evokes a wide range of images: a sweet little old lady in a country village to whom everyone comes with their ailments; a preacher at a Hallelujah-shouting revivalist tent meeting in the Bible Belt of America, a Filipino psychic surgeon removing tumours, a New Age mystic with a crystal.

But then, how about these: a six-foot-four American Ivy League scholar and athlete, the personal aide to a European monarch, a British military officer?

Which group are the healers? Though there are undoubtedly individuals like those in the first group who are healers, the second group are real people who perform healings, and one, the American, does it as a profession.

WHAT HEALING IS

Healing means recovery. As the word is normally used, healing is regaining vitality, 'getting well'. When used in the metaphysical sense, 'the touch', as healing is sometimes called, refers to the improvement of a condition, physical or otherwise, at a pace or in a manner beyond what is considered realistically possible. But in the metaphysical realm, the unexpected can be an everyday event.

Healing normally has results such as the loss of pain, disappearance of symptoms, the restoration of function; all accomplished in a manner that logic and modern medicine are at a loss to explain. Whatever healing is, whoever does it, and however it is done, one thing is sure – it has been around for a long time.

The job of healer was an important one in very early societies. In addition to caring for the sick and injured, the healer was the 'medicine man' (or woman) who held the lore of the remedies, trained students, and passed on knowledge. To the eye of the man of the time, a healer was the possessor of magical skills. And perhaps he was. With all their intellectual theories and tests, scientists are today no more sure exactly what happens when healing takes place than were the earliest people.

WHERE HEALING HAPPENS

Healing occurs in the dimension beyond the physical. Though the effects we can *see* are usually in the physical body, healing can equally result in a change of a condition to the mental, or the emotional, nature. It will relieve the pain of a burn, but it can as easily soften the blow of a traumatic shock, such as an unexpected death. By the use of means not visible to the eye, healing engages a force or energy from the non-physical realms. The source and nature of this force, who can use it and how they are able to access it, and what it affects to get the results it does are the cause of debate, argument and research among scientists. Fortunately this lack of proper scientific validation has not stopped healers, who continue in their variety of guises and using a bewildering range of techniques to keep on doing what they're good at – healing.

One thing all healers do have in common is their intention. No matter what the technique used or the background of the healer, it is vital that the intention is that there will be a change for the better. It is not, however, necessarily conscious. Many of us use healing energy in this unconscious manner when those we care about are ill or uncomfortable. A simple caress, a hand on a shoulder or even a loving gaze sends healing energy to the recipient.

WHAT IS IT THAT HAS THE POWER TO HEAL?

Chi. Prana. Ka. These are the words for healing energy in the ancient language of China, India and Egypt, respectively. These terms are each culture's way of expressing the non-physical force which moves when healing occurs. Healers can sense this type of energy, as can most recipients. Usually it feels warm, both to the healer and the recipient, and sometimes it is tingly, even when the healer's hands don't physically touch the body.

You can experience the feeling of this healing energy. Perhaps the easiest way is by rubbing the palm of the hands together, rapidly, as if warming them up after coming in out of the cold, until there is a feeling of heat in them. Then hold the palms up facing each other separated by a couple of inches. Move them gradually closer, until there is a feeling of warmth and a sense almost like a cushion between them. Pull the palms slowly apart and see if this sensation disappears, then bring them together again noting when you can feel the energy. It is this sort of energy which is mobilised in healing. We all have the capacity to produce it. It is the process of healing which calls on this energy and the healer who activates and directs it.

WHERE DOES THE ENERGY GO?

In healing, it appears that the healer is sending energy to the recipient. The healer's hands become warm, and there is a strong feeling of the transfer of energy. Yet the majority of healers feel it is not their own personal energy which is being employed in this process. Some feel they draw on a universal pool of energy which is there for the asking.

Once directed to the recipient, energies from the outside work on the subject. But because not all effects from healing occur immediately, some unfolding over days or even weeks, it is difficult to say if it is the healing energy brought from the outside alone which gets the results, or if it mobilises energy from within which the subject continues to use. Many healers themselves are not sure exactly what does happen. What is certain is a change called healing does occur as the result of the presence of this force.

WHO HEALS?

Is someone who has healing powers part way to sainthood? Many assume one would have to be at least a little bit better than the average person to be able to heal. Yet it appears that everyone, not only healers, has access to the energy which is used in healing. You've felt it yourself. The warm energy created in your palms can be directed to others. The ability to do that can be enhanced by study. But it does seem that healers start out with a greater capacity to call on and send out this special energy.

Does this mean they are holier than the rest of us? While the ability to heal is one of the characteristics of great souls and saints, there are some very ordinary human beings who have the power to channel healing energy.

If healers are special in any way, it is because they care enough about others to make the effort to learn how to use the healing energy for others' benefit. With some notable exceptions, healing is not a career anyone goes into to get rich. If there is something special to be admired about healers, it is their willingness to give their time and attention to the welfare of others.

Though everyone has the potential to heal, the ability does seem to run in families. Whether this is because the children grow up and see adults using the energy and imitate them and learn, or it is a hereditary skill, is difficult to say. But in cultures all over the world it is recognised that some families have 'the touch'.

Yet some who have the power to use healing energy did not grow up in surroundings where they saw others doing it. An example of this is the well-known and much-studied English healer Matthew Manning, who was raised in a household with little background in any metaphysical area. When he was in his teens, frequent and very extreme poltergeist activity, such all the furniture in an unoccupied room piling itself up against the door, understandably drew attention to him. Eventually experts on the paranormal were able to determine how and why the family home had suddenly become such a vortex of activity, but it took some time to ascertain that it was Matthew's powers which were the cause. This discovery led to the scientific study of Matthew's considerable psychical abilities, in a wide variety of experiments conducted in the UK and USA. Some years of such testing led Matthew himself to begin to explore the use of his powers for healing others. He now devotes his time to healing and to helping others discover their own abilities as well.

HEALING HISTORY

The original medicine man, or the shaman, as he was also called, was in early times doctor, healer and often priest. As societies became more complex and duties were divided, the priestly tasks went to others and the shaman became a full-time keeper of ritual wisdom and tender of the sick. At that time it was considered that all illness, be they mental, spiritual, emotional or physical, came from the same source, a loss connection with the deity. Because people could not recognise germs or viruses, a bout of influenza was viewed as a condition no different from a psychological depression. It was the healer's job to bring the patient back into a healthy state by restoring that connection with the divine energy. The source of the separation was believed to have a variety of causes: it could be a curse from another, or something the individual did himself to cause separation from the deity.

Later, it was understood that particular remedies could be used to heal certain conditions and the first ideas about medicine were beginning to take form, so the relationship between herbs and the recovery from disease became established. Yet it was still necessary for the shaman to administer the remedy; in the eyes of the patient it was faith in the healer, not the substance administered, which made the healing occur.

FAITH HEALING

This brings up one of the greatest puzzles in the mystery of how healing works, and one of the major issues for healers today; faith healing. How much of what occurs when healing happens is the result of belief on the part of the patient?

The sovereigns of England and France were once credited with the power to heal. As the conduit of God's wisdom and power, it is not surprising that the king was also empowered with this ability. In the Middle Ages, Edward the Confessor, who was canonised for his saintliness, was credited with the ability to heal scrofula, the sores which accompany tuberculosis, which was endemic at the time. By the seventeenth century there were organised healing receptions to which thousands of subjects came. But the condition which the king specialised in healing was one which tended to disappear spontaneously anyway. Could the king's touch alone precipitate that kind of healing?

The line where faith enters the picture in healing is no more clearly drawn than it is in medicine. Doctors have conducted experiments over the years to try to differentiate the impact of faith in medication by using a placebo, a substance which has no actual physical effect on the body. In numerous experiments, it has been shown that the simple faith of patients in the medications they are given by their consultants, even if they are placebos, will result in a change in their condition, if not in healing.

This does not mean that all healing is the result of simple faith alone, however. As easy as it would be to draw that conclusion, an experiment done with American healer Olga Worrall, which tested the effect of her attentions, suggests that is not the case. The subject in this case was not as likely to be swayed by faith as a person – it was rye-grass. After measuring the growth rate of the grass in the laboratory without treatments, it was sent energy by Worrall. The ryegrass grew 775 per cent more rapidly in the day after it was 'healed'. The growth slowed in the days thereafter, but never slowed to the original pace. This impressive result on the ryegrass, not an easily suggestible subject, indicates that in some situations, at least, something does happen in healing.

There is a second aspect to the experiment mentioned. At the time she performed the healing, the ryegrass was in Atlanta, in the state of Georgia, and Worrall was in Baltimore, Maryland, some several hundred miles away. The term for this is remote healing. Healers can send their energy to a person (or a plant, apparently) a great distance away as easily as to someone near to them. As with so many aspects of the realm of metaphysics, it seems that distance is no limitation in healing.

CLASSIFYING HEALING

The goal of healing is the improvement of the condition of the subject. Under the umbrella of healing comes a range of activities which includes everything from a friendly but healing pat on the back, the simple hands-on transfer of healing energy, the gradual healing of a chronic condition, remote healing, to psychic surgery.

Psychic surgery is one of the most controversial and potentially dangerous areas of this extended realm of healing. Often in the press there are reports of 'doctors' who operate in filthy conditions, with the most appalling of instruments, without anaesthesia, yet who can in a flash remove tumours and correct complex medical conditions. Investigations have proved many of these are just as worthy of suspicion as they sound. Fraudulently, they do not (probably fortunately) actually open up the body, but use trickery to make it appear that they do surgery and to produce the blood and the 'tumours' they remove. If you hear of a 'healer' who works this way, this is not the time for naive trust or experimentation, particularly if there is a serious medical condition involved. Do not abandon conventional medical treatment for a healer whose cures you have been told are 'miraculous'.

Yet there are a few exceptions, healers of this type whose activities have survived the most thorough investigations. One element these have in common is that they have a connection with the 'other side', so they have some help from guides or entities who assist them. A particularly fascinating tale of this sort involves a 'psychic' healer and surgeon who became extremely well-known in his home country of Brazil.

At the age of 30, the poorly educated Minas Gerias began having episodes of depression and disorientation. He consulted a spiritualist who told him this was caused because a spirit was trying to come through him. The spirit was that of a German doctor, Adolphus Fritz. Allowing the doctor to work through him, Gerias, who came to be known as Arigo, became a phenomenon in Brazil in the 1950s and 1960s. Though still uneducated, he effectively treated hundreds of cases with surgery and prescriptions of drugs. He said the voice in his head told him what to do and what drugs to order. In the 1960s the medical establishment finally cracked down on this popular hero and he was brought to trial for practising medicine without a licence. As popular and well known as his work was, it was not possible to defend him legally as it was rather difficult to *prove* that the real doctor, the spirit of Dr Adolphus Fritz, who directed Arigo in what he did, was present when Arigo worked with patients. Reluctantly, the judge found Arigo guilty. He went to prison, where he continued to see his patients as the warden would not lock the door of his cell, and he was released after six months when the governor pardoned him. His career ended suddenly when Arigo was killed in a car crash in 1971, plunging Brazil into mourning for their beloved healer.

The German doctor Fritz did not give up easily, though he had obviously learned a lesson; this time he chose an already accredited and practising physician to work through.

In 1980, still in Brazil, Dr Edson de Quieroz began to receive the guidance of Dr Fritz. Dr Quieroz has carried on Arigo's healing work, though he still practises conventional medicine at his own clinic as well. He says he is not only assisted by Fritz, but by a team of over a thousand spirits with a wide variety of specialities, all of whom were doctors when they were alive on earth.

TYPES OF HEALING

By now it is obvious that the word healing embraces a wide range of techniques. The original role of healer, the medicine man or shaman, has been expanded over the ages. With a technique as subjective as healing, it is not easy to make distinctions between methods, but there are some clear differences.

Shamanistic Altered-state healing which derives from the most ancient techniques. Also uses ritual, herbs, trance, chanting.

Spiritual Channels healing energy to the subject, not directing it specifically, but allowing it to go in wherever is necessary. **Remote** spiritual healing energy is directed from a distance.

Laying on of hands Using spiritual energy for healing while actually touching the body, usually a target area.

Faith Healing in a setting where the belief of the participants is emphasised. Occurs in all religions.

Spiritual healers Trained healers in Great Britain who use energy to bring comfort and relief to the ill.

Therapeutic Touch American-originated technique developed by a nurse for use with patients, emphasises the power of healing.

Miracles The sudden and inexplicable curing of a condition, usually as the result of apparent intervention by a divine agent.

Self-healing Mobilises the healing forces from within.

Visualisation Using the imaging powers of the mind to activate healing within the body.

Christian Science Religion which uses meditation and study of the scriptures, as well as belief of unreality of the physical, as an approach to healing (often accompanied by a trained practitioner).

TYPES OF HEALERS

Every healer uses the same energy. When they heal, even if briefly, they 'centre' themselves, turning inward and becoming aligned with the higher realms from which healing energy comes. Every healer desires to bring positive results. Beyond that there is a world of techniques, approaches and intellectual explanations about how to heal and what happens.

People who are healers have arrived at their work in an assortment of ways. Some just do it with friends, without thinking much about it. Those who have grown up around healing may never formally train. Others study with teachers who have a specific technique, or learn it because of their work. Some come to it through their religious studies. Others don't believe in God at all, but like the way they feel when healing. There is no standard path to be a healer, nor is there a single way to learn about it.

Healers work in different ways, too. There are several states the healer can be in when healing. He can be in an altered state, as Dr Quieroz would when he receives counsel from his spiritual 'medical board'. In this state he suspends his ordinary day-to-day awareness in order to 'tune in' to information from other realms. He is still conscious and able to talk to others. A few healers will go into a trance when they work and recall nothing of what they did or said. Others, such as nurses using Therapeutic Touch, work in a state of 'centred' but waking consciousness, calling on the healing energies, concentrating on what they are doing, still easily able to cope with distractions.

197

RESULTS OF HEALING

When people first enter the world of healing, they think the goal must surely be the *cure* of a condition. There is a difference between healing and curing. A cure ends the presence of a condition, as well as its symptoms. While there have been a notable number of cures from catastrophic conditions, such as cancer, as the result of healing, some with the attendance of a doctor, there is still no way to assure consistent results of this kind from healing. A cure such as this is really more a miracle, a special sort of healing.

The goal of healing is the relief of pain, the ease of distress, the lifting of the spirit. The result of healing is sometimes a more rapid recovery from a condition or illness, diminished symptoms, easing of pain. Some healing is used to enhance conventional medical treatments, or to allay side-effects, such as those which occur in chemo-therapy. When they work most healers direct the healing energy in a non-specific manner, that is with the intention that it serve in whatever way it is needed.

Because healing uses energy which flows to the point where it is most needed, not only are its results not always immediately apparent, but the area it first affects may not be the reason the healing was requested. For example, someone may ask for a healer to work on relieving the pain of a chronically troubled tummy, an early sign of an ulcer. Though following the consultant's medical advice, the subject may want to speed along his recovery. Having weekly healings, it may be discovered that, as the distress of his stomach is disappearing, his relationship with his wife is also improving as the result of the healings. As the stress of this may have been the cause of the condition to start with, the healing energy went where it was most needed – to the relationship.

PROOF

The fact that the goal of healers is relief, not a cure, confounds scientists who like to have absolutes to measure in their experiments. While the production of healing energy and its effect can be measured scientifically, measurable *results* are more elusive. Experimenters are not satisfied with a patient saying 'I feel better', if they can't measure how much better.

If you have ever had the experience of being healed, you have the knowledge of the difference in the feeling before and after. Whether it was in a formal situation, attended to by a healer, or the simple gesture of a friend, perhaps relieving the pain of a headache, you know the shift of energy which accompanies healing.

One girl experienced this when she was unwise enough to go barefoot near her boyfriend's large and heavily shod feet. Not watching where he was stepping, he trod on her toe. Very few things hurt as much as a stubbed toe, and she hopped and moaned with pain; he surprised her when he not only apologised profusely, but used healing energy on her. He put his hand on her foot and the pain stopped immediately and never returned. She thought it was just one of those incredibly painful toes which hurts horribly, but only for a little while. But it had been so badly crushed that a few weeks later the whole nail fell off. The healing had relieved her of the pain, though the tissue of the toe had remained severely damaged.

MEDICINE AND HEALING

About one hundred years ago there was a break between the worlds of science and medicine, and traditional healing. Healing is regarded as unsubstantial by much of the medical establishment, having been grouped together with the ideas and techniques now called 'New Age'. Though most of the New Age techniques go back in history farther than medicine itself, because many of them do not respond well to conventional scientific testing, they are not as yet regarded as reliable techniques by doctors.

In spite of this reluctance healing techniques are beginning to return to medicine. The relatively new field of psychoneuro-immunology (PNI) explores the connection of the mind, the nervous system and the immune system in keeping us healthy and preventing illness and disease. Though PNI specialists are still challenged in their experiments to *prove* that the state of mind actually influences the wellbeing of the body, some acknowledge 'deep down' that they know such influences exist.

Self-healing combined with traditional medicine appears to be a powerful combination. The power of visualisation has been applied in a variety of situations with significant results. One of the earliest was the use of such imagery at the Simonton Clinic for Treatment of Cancer in Texas. Working with patients with severe conditions who were undergoing conventional medical treatment as well, the Simontons directed the participants to see the effects of their radiation or chemotherapy weakening the cancer cells and allowing the body's own immune system cells, the lymphocytes, to win and carry away the dead cancer cells. Dramatic imagery was encouraged; patients would produce pictures such as seeing their white cells as powerful warriors overcoming the villain cancer cells in a drama taking place in their own bodies. The Simontons' technique extended both the vitality and survival time of their patients, the goal in treating this sort of cancer.

PNI researchers are exploring the idea that there is a power to heal within each of us, which, when mobilised by need, belief or visualisation, vitalises the immune system. In addition, in individual situations self-healing is now being used to help heal injuries and broken bones more quickly, to aid physiotherapy, and to enable nutritional and vitamin therapies to work efficiently.

Remembering that the purpose of healing is improving the condition of the subject, the relief of symptoms, the restoration of function, and not necessarily obtaining a cure, it becomes increasingly possible to anticipate that its techniques will be able to be more frequently used to enhance medical treatments in the future.

When you decide to go for a healing session, it is not even necessary to know exactly what you want. As healing energy can be directed to go where it is most needed, those areas will pull the energy to them. Of course, there may be a particular matter which you want treated, in which case it can be discussed with the healer and requested as the focus of the session.

There is no predictable timetable with healing. On occasion there might be an immediate response to treatment, but normally the shift is more subtle and comes over time. Healing is a process and will often require more than one visit.

Fees for healing are usually modest. A few healers do not like to accept money; if that is the case it is appropriate to bring them simple gifts from time to time as an acknowledgement of your thanks.

It is essential that you feel absolutely comfortable with a healer. Be sure to ask questions as they come up, both about the condition you are there for, if there is a specific one, and the techniques being used. It is important to feel free to ask any question and get a satisfactory answer, and to feel trust in what the healer says.

In order to approach healing intelligently, take time to consider the integrity of the healer. Unfortunately, there are frauds in the field, both the dramatic 'psychic surgeon' and the innocuous but perhaps more dangerous types who gain confidence while emptying your bank account.

The warnings in the case of the 'psychic surgery' type are all too clear. Be suspicious. While there are remarkable individuals who have been trained in techniques beyond those that medicine dreams of today, they are rare and, in most cases, keep to themselves, working very privately. Consider the source of a practitioner of this sort, note if there is a calm attitude around them or a hysteria.

More subtle forms of fraud occur in a New Age version of the confidence scheme. Difficult to detect, because the presentation may not be so dramatically suspicious, the things to beware of are promises a bit too good to be true and veiled threats. If promised a cure, told medication is no longer necessary, told not to see your medical consultant anymore, threatened, told that without treatments your condition will worsen, that a series of appointments must be purchased in advance, confront the healer with your suspicions and queries. If you do not get satisfactory answers, run, do not walk, to the police. Reputable healers do not want the few people of this sort ruining the hard work they are doing to make healing better known and understood. You will help them by reporting these unscrupulous people who would take advantage of others.

No healer will ever recommend abandoning conventional medical treatment or medication. The movies where the healed drop their crutches at their sides as they rise to their feet are dramas, not reality. Miraculous healings are possible, and are reported from time to time. Because they do happen sometimes is no reason to abandon conventional treatment.

DO-IT-YOURSELF HEALING

Healing is one area of metaphysical techniques you can share. You can use your own healing energy, sending it to others.

It is interesting to attend a class in healing (most likely offered through a local bookstore or centre specialising in metaphysical subjects), but healing power can safely be explored on your own. Having discovered what it feels like, you can practise on a friend. Ask them to report what they feel when you direct healing energy to them. It is also possible to experiment with remote healing.

There are some techniques and precautions which should be observed. If working on someone who has an illness or pain, be careful not to take on the symptoms of their condition as you heal them. It is easy for a beginner to do so. Before beginning healing, imagine a shield protecting you from their ailment. Visualise the energy coming out of you but not returning from them. It is also important not to take responsibility for the subject 'getting better'. Healing is fundamentally an act of love, giving without expectation of return. When the ego gets in the picture, healing becomes forced. Let the healing energy go where it is most needed, rather than trying to decide what and how to heal.

Also try self-healing. Though not a substitute for proper medical attention, it can advance the healing of any condition or healing energy can be used to relax the body so it can mend.

Healing energy is limitless. It never hurts to circulate it, with the intention of benefiting the recipient. You can use it with the assurance that it will find the proper destination without your needing to supervise its arrival. Every warm loving thought sent to another contains a dose of healing energy. There can never be too much of that in today's world.

15

Magic, Ritual and Spells

Haven't there been times when each of us would have happily had a curse put on someone? Perhaps on the girl who pinched your first boyfriend? On a noisy neighbour? Or have you ever wished for a potion to charm your bank manager? The idea of being able to use the power of the magical for your own purposes is probably both fascinating and absolutely terrifying. And quite properly, too.

But then you've never had anything to do with ritual magic, anyway. There are sensational stories about people who have gotten involved with spells and witchcraft. But before you congratulate yourself for having avoided that, cast back in your mind and think: have you ever lit a candle in church for a sick friend, tossed a coin in a well and made a wish, talked to a picture of a loved one as if you were speaking to them? Then you, too, have done magic. These are all simple spells. Yes, magic. Each of these activities uses a symbolic object or gift or image (the candle, the coin, the photo) as a focus to ask to have a task accomplished by magical means. The act (the lighting of the candle, the tossing of the coin, the talking to the picture) and the intention behind it are the components of the sort of magic discussed here. The first two, lighting the candle and tossing the coin, are rituals, familiar to us all; the latter is called sympathetic magic, which uses an object as a symbol for another person, in this case, a photograph.

MAGIC

The magic discussed here, let us be clear, is not the magic of rabbits popping out of hats, and ladies being sawn in half. Skilled art though that is, we do not find it in the land of metaphysics because it manipulates the *physical* world to make it *appear* that the laws of nature have been altered. A magician in this sense creates the illusion that the physical world laws have been suspended when indeed they have not. A magician of this sort is even called an illusionist, or prestidigitator, which means manipulator.

In the type of magic explored here, the laws of nature themselves *are* temporarily altered by the use of ritual; magical techniques are used to accomplish the practitioner's goals.

Of all of the realms of the land of metaphysics, this one carries the greatest sense of the mystery of pure power. While there is no question that many of the individuals and some of the techniques of this realm are truly chilling, there are others which are affirmations of the force and glory of nature as used by those truly aligned with its principles. Indeed, in this land, the range of ethics is great and so is the need for knowledge and assessment on the part of the visitor. In this realm too is perhaps one of the most alluring temptations of any kingdom – the capacity to have power not only over nature, but over another person.

Yet here also lies the ability to form a relationship with the elements of the earth in a way few of us do today. By becoming familiar with these laws, the magician not only masters them, but also honours them.

The technique used in this kind of magic is usually a spell. A spell is a binding agreement made by the magician with forces and elements of nature which compels

205

a particular event to occur. It can affect any aspect of life from nature, as with a Rain Dance done by Red Indians, to a spell to change another's behaviour. A spell not in the best interests of another is called a curse.

Magicians have as many names as there are cultures in which they exist. In addition to the familiar witch, warlock, shaman, sorcerer, witch doctor and high priest or priestess, there are the Hawaiian kahuna, and the Haitian Voodoo macumba, and the African-derived Caribbean obeah.

In England in particular, magic is associated with witchcraft. While witchcraft certainly is one aspect of the magical art, the image of the witch with her bubbling cauldron and black cat is a misleading one, not only in terms of modern-day witches in Great Britain, but in terms of what the word magic embraces in its larger sense.

Magic is much misunderstood, and any cause not within the range of logical reality tends to be considered as magical. For example, many medicines that were thought to be magical no longer are because scientific investigation has unveiled how they work. In one instance, the bark and roots of the willow, a 'magical cure' for fever and headaches among the Red Indians, and recommended by Hippocrates, the founder of medicine as a science, has been discovered to have in it salicylic acid, a component of aspirin. Now the source of its power is understood, it is no longer magical, just ordinary medicine.

Anything which transcends the way reality is understood seems magical until explained. To the illiterate peasant of medieval times, the theatrical effects of travelling miracle plays, with actors going up in puffs of smoke and disappearing from the centre of the stage, were complete magic. For the players it was their craft and all in a day's work. For many of us today the way a computer works seems magical, yet to computer programmers, it's very simple and direct.

For the sorcerer or magician, magic is not the world of the unexplained, but a very serious study indeed. It is the world of nature, and the rituals used to invoke its powers; equally it is the world of spirit, and rituals to invoke their wisdom. A true magician approaches this practice with reverence and humility. Magic has the potential to dominate not only nature, but others, and the magician must use it wisely, with the understanding that he carries with him teachings reaching back to earliest man.

There are magicians the world over. They can be male or female. They are not limited to peculiar headdress and carrying rattling ritual relics; they could just as easily appear wearing a business suit or cocktail dress. What they have in common is that they have studied under a magician themselves and have passed at least one test of initiation. No one gets to be a magician of power by reading a book. While someone who has studied, but is uninitiated, can cast a spell of some degree, or make a ritual, the sort of serious spell within the powers of a full magician takes knowledge, experience, and reverence.

There is a tendency today to divide magic neatly into two paths, referred to as 'black' magic and 'white' magic. White magic is meant not to interfere with the free will of others, while magic of the black sort does. For example, a spell done to get more money would be considered white magic, but a spell to make your employer give you a rise in pay would be 'black' magic, as you would be interfering with free will. As with all simplistic definitions, this rather misses the point. *All* magic manipulates the energies of the world and those in it. The powers available are huge and the potential for indirect results from apparently simple actions is great; this is why training is given to very few, is very rigorous and the final keys are handed over only when tests of strength and of character are passed. An inept magician not only risks interfering with the free will of others, he risks the balance of nature and his own welfare.

Most of the more publicly visible magicians, both 'black' and 'white', do not wield the power of those who have undergone this sort of training.

THE TRAINING

For the student, the decision to undertake training in magic is the easiest part of the process. Finding a true teacher and being accepted is considerably more of a challenge. Once the relationship between teacher and student is formed, a path opens which has not changed for millennia.

Whether the teacher is South American, Balinese or Tibetan, the organisation of the student's training will be similar. When he (or she, for there are many females who have pursued this study) arrives, he will be made welcome by the teacher and by fellow students. Soon afterwards the teacher will ask why he has come. Though his intentions may seem obvious, especially as many of the places where great teachers live are rather out of the way, and take considerable effort to reach, the question is not an idle enquiry. Before the student begins his studies, he must ask to be taught. It is then that the teacher formally accepts him or her.

In the beginning the student is generally either ignored by the teacher or given tasks which seem unimportant. This is designed not only to test the student's sincerity, but to reduce the ego so that training can really begin. Tales of students' early torments are very amusing to read, but probably weren't much fun to endure. A wise teacher is well able to select the exact activity which will arouse the portion of the student's ego needing reduction. An example would be a very intellectual student who has studied a great deal to impress the teacher with his preparation, who will likely end up peeling potatoes or tilling soil for two weeks, or as long as it takes for the fact-filled mind to stop thinking that it is quite so important.

Then begins the real training. Teachers must impart to their students knowledge of magical materials, of beings from other planes, of ritual, power, and responsibility. At this level of magic, an incorrect choice can boomerang awfully. So a student may be sent out five times to collect wood for a ritual fire until the proper kind of wood is found. And the teacher may not even tell the student what the proper kind of wood looks like, but will just send him out again and again until he learns to *see* and sense for himself what is correct.

In this process, every element of magical lore is thus learned. The student either finds out himself what to do, with the close, though not always visible, supervision of his teacher, or learns by watching and imitating as the teacher performs magical acts, or listening to tales of the teacher's own training and experience.

Some students stay with their teachers until their studies are completed; others come and go as they may have interests in the world they must maintain. Some drop out.

Along the way there will be tests, small examples of the final rites of initiation the student can expect at the culmination of his studies. Often a test of this sort will require the student to find a personal object of power or to face an inner or an outer adversary on his own. An example of this is common among all North American Indian initiations: the student must spend the night out in the open awaiting contact with his animal counterpart, normally a wild animal that the uninitiated would find simply terrifying. The student must greet this animal with steadfast courage. At this point a few more decide these studies are no longer to their taste or simply fail.

Eventually, after what may be years of study, it is time for the final initiation. It is the point where the teacher feels the student has absorbed everything he is able, and all that the teacher has to pass on.

The final initiation is complex. It usually includes a

number of tasks, some on the physical plane, others dealing with the spirit realm. An example of the physical sort is the test given to Tibetan lamas: they must sit alone in the snow of the Himalayas and be able to make it melt in a circle for six feet around them.

The time, commitment and complexity of the training of a magician suggests that the ranks of initiates of great power are not likely to swell rapidly.

RITUAL POWER AND SPELLS

In order to approach the world of ritual power, the world of spells and those who cast them, either to avail yourself of those powers, or to study them, you must have knowledge of where their power comes from and what they employ to get their results. This power is most seductive, and possibly dangerous – to the uninformed.

Though this is not a chapter on satanism, it must be mentioned with a caution here. Satan is viewed as the Dark God and intentions of most of those who follow this path are not orientated to the good and wellbeing of others. The satanic rituals call forth the specific powers which feed off this sort of dark energy. As in every aspect of the land of metaphysics, there is no activity which is without its effect, and even exploring this out of simple curiosity can have unpleasant results. Once entangled with the web of these powers, it is not simple to extricate oneself.

Some of it may seem so innocent. What could be wrong with the odd spell here and there, what's a potion among friends? Yet even at this point discrimination is essential. The most innocent-seeming spell may begin a pattern of the seduction of power and obligation. Sometimes it is easier simply to ask for what you want.

RITUALS

Life is full of rituals. Some are rites of passage, and seem so familiar that we don't especially think of them as ritual. For most of us, the wedding ceremony with the bride appearing veiled in white is a very familiar ritual indeed. We all know the order of events and know that when the ritual is completed the couple will be considered married. And we believe it is the ritual, not the registering of the marriage, which makes the couple truly wed. Other rituals are foreign to us and may seem quite strange.

Rituals not associated with religion are usually considered superstitions. An actor who cannot go on stage without a drink of water, uses the water as a ritual rather than to satisfy thirst. A student who must wear socks of a certain colour and heads for a particular corner of the room in an examination is behaving in a ritualistic manner. 'Superstitions' though they may be, because of repeated use, these actions become rituals. Over the years they become so familiar that we think of them as neither ritual nor magical but as traditions. This sort of tradition is exemplified by the kissing of the Blarney Stone, the ritual said to give the gifts of charm and gab. A ritual can be performed to protect or to avoid an unfortunate result as well, such as the tossing of spilled salt over the shoulder.

Ritual is done to invoke power, or protect, as is the case in a blessing; or to make something happen, as in the Red Indian Rain Dance. Most rituals are quite innocent and are perfectly safe. The individual who conducts the ritual calls on and gathers together the forces of spirit or of nature to achieve the results commanded. Rituals can bless, command and create.

ELEMENTS OF RITUAL

The formula of a ritual is called a spell. No matter how large or small, formal ritual must contain certain elements. It must have symbols, relevant to the culture in which it is being performed. It must evoke the senses – sound, smell, sight and touch or movement. The individual conducting it must maintain a state of focused attention throughout. It must have a clear beginning and end.

Ritual is used in many situations and to a wide variety of ends. We tend to consider familiar rituals as normal, those of foreign cultures as superstition or pagan. All of these, no matter the culture, are used to mark transitional events such as weddings, christenings and funerals. Those used in 'primitive' cultures are also used to evoke powers to ensure a good harvest, to heal, or to protect livestock.

Rituals use symbols. Symbols are objects or images which mean something beyond their direct use. A horseshoe is only a shoe for a horse when it's on the hoof; over a doorway, it is a symbol of luck. Rituals involving other people often use a symbol for that person. This is called sympathetic magic. Ideally something from the person's physical body is used, such as a lock of hair; a possession can be used, or even a picture of the individual. In the absence of any of those, an object is given the identity of the subject, usually a doll. This is the origin of the legendary 'voodoo doll'. The method has long been used in England as well, with centuries-old 'poppet' dolls still preserved in museums.

SPELLS

Who can forget the movie *Fantasia*, with Mickey Mouse as the unfortunate sorcerer's apprentice? Lazy Mickey, told to fetch water by his departing master, thought it easier to give one of master's spells a try. Finding the right one, he enchanted a broom to do his fetching for him, while Mickey relaxed. Relaxed, that is, until the now animated broom's productivity began to flood his master's rooms. Unable to find the spell to *turn off* his slave, he smashed the broom to bits, only to see each piece leap up and continue to carry on his bidding! Just moments before all the contents of the room, including the terrified Mickey, were about to float away the sorcerer appeared to save the situation with the spell to stop the flow.

Rituals, and spells, which are a kind of ritual, have been restricted to the initiated because of their potential power. As poor Mickey found out, a little knowledge, especially of a spell, is a very dangerous thing!

A spell is cast in a special kind of ritual. The purpose of a spell is to call the powers of a particular deity, or of nature, to perform a task. But the inexperienced caster of spells invites disaster. This is why the casting of spells of any degree of power is reserved only for those who have studied and been initiated.

There are a few basic sorts of spells. One type is meant to protect. Examples of these are the familiar blessings which are part of any religion. Blessings of worshippers, blessings of couples being married, of small children, of possessions such as homes, or in the countryside, livestock, are common everywhere in the world.

Other spells are meant to invoke a situation or a condition. They call on the appropriate powers and ask them to fulfil the request. People having backyard barbecues would love to have a rain-prevention ritual. These spells address the forces of nature, the elementals, the beings who guide nature's aspects. By appealing to the elementals of the weather, the caster of the spell can request any weather condition desired. There is a report of an Indian shaman who wanted the dusty earth tamped down by a light shower before he performed a ritual, but a heavier one to remove the footmarks of the dances after the ritual was completed. He asked the rain elementals to do this for him and to the amazement of the student reporting the event, he got exactly as much rain as he wanted when he wanted it.

Everyone has heard of the spells of the Caribbean, the spells of Voodoo. There are tales of those who have had a spell put on them intended to make them die and have just simply died, with no apparent medical cause; and tales of zombies, the undead state, where the body and will are taken over by the sorcerer's power. Stories such as these abound in regions where ritual magic is used as an ordinary part of the culture as opposed to those more 'civilised' countries where ritual magic has been replaced by scientific magic.

In the cultures of the Caribbean Islands and Brazil, the powers of the magicians, usually called obeahs or macumbahs, are an important part of daily life, but other cultures are also familiar with the role of magic. Writings on such a diverse range of places such as India, Tibet, Hawaii, Peru, Mexico, Russia, and of course Africa, whence came the tradition which has become known as Voodoo, report events in which individuals have been both helped, healed of illness, or have been enchanted or cursed, in some cases, indeed, to the point of death. This may sound extreme, if not ridiculous, to our ears, yet the tales of this sort of event are consistent from a variety of authoritative sources over a long period of time.

Spells can be done to affect the physical plane. They can be done to influence, to protect oneself or to attack another. They can be done to affect other people's wellbeing or to influence their free will and behaviour.

The working of spells is serious business. Before running off to your local macumbah, remember that St Theresa commented that more tears are shed over answered prayers than over anything else. With magic, the first law is to be careful not only about what you want, but to be aware of the effects which can occur as a result of the method used on your behalf. If, after such warnings, you are still spell shopping, here is a list of what's on offer.

KINDS OF SPELLS

Physical world
Calls on the powers to act on your instructions to do the following:
    Protection
        Blessing of home, family, self

Property
Business
For times of danger, travel, any risk

Acquisition
Money
Power
Honour
Property

Physical body
Sexual potency
Fertility – children (and of the desired sex)
Physical strength
Health, protection from disease
Youthfulness

Nature
Calls on the nature elementals to produce the specific desired effect:
Fertility
Crops
Livestock
Weather (dry or wet)

Over others
If there is something which edges more towards black magic, it is that which encroaches on the free will of others. Be aware.

Love
Love potions (to get them to love you)
Binding spells (to keep them there)
Control
Enchantment
Attack (these are called curses)
Spells to weaken or kill
Damage property or goods

Charms
Using objects of power blessed to a purpose.
Protection
Power

THE POWER OF BELIEF

When entering the realm of magic, most rationally educated people will suggest that it is the belief in the power of the practitioner of magic that makes the spell work. Psychologists call this reaction to belief 'self-fulfilling prophecy'. For example, the client of a reader, perhaps, of the Tarot, may have been told that a fight at home is coming; they then go home and live out the prediction by having a spat. This sort of psychological approach says that believers in magic are similarly subject to the powers of the magician simply because of their belief. While this is undoubtedly sometimes the case, there are too many documented situations where either the subject of a spell or curse has been unaware of its being cast, and still responded, or where the spell has been over the powers of nature, to discount completely the effects of the spell on this basis.

THE POWER OF THE MIND

Much of a magician's training has to do with focusing the mind. Ritual is ineffective at mustering the forces of nature to do its bidding without the clear intention behind it. We have all willed things to come to pass, been surprised when they actually happen, then quickly discounted the connection between the focus of our intentions and the resulting event. That connection is the foundation of thought in the entire land of metaphysics.

An interesting aspect of the power of the mind in witchcraft is that spells are returnable. Just because a spell has been done and has been sent along to the subject, the subject does not need to accept it. In order to protect themselves, most people who are knowledgeable about magic do not easily give away their picture or other possessions, and keep themselves very centred and self-aware. The more disorganised the character of the subject, the more muddied the psyche by the excessive use of substances such as alcohol or drugs, the less likely the subject will be able to repel the spell. Being surrounded by those who love you is an excellent protection from any evil spell as well.

Few ever get a view of the workings of an initiated magician. Those who have met one or seen one in action always report being impressed by the power, presence, and focus they have as an individual, and, perhaps surprisingly, their sense of humour.

WITCHCRAFT IN ENGLAND

The United Kingdom has a very ancient tradition of magical practices. The evidence of stone circles, such as Stonehenge, of which there are some 500 spread across Great Britain, as well as the sacred wells, of which there are an equal number, testify to the abundance of activity in olden times. The Druidic religion associated with these sites observed the earlier nature religions. Some of these were incorporated into the Druids' rituals.

The story of Merlin, King Arthur's teacher, whether it is historically true or not, points out a history of this kind of study over the centuries. Merlin was a trained magician, called a wizard. He had tremendous powers and knowledge and trained the young King Arthur, using his powers to see the problems Arthur would encounter in the future and to prepare him for them. Equally, there is the tradition of the village 'wise woman', who could be relied upon as a healer, but whom it was not a good idea to cross.

Today there are many who practise witchcraft as an aspect of the Druidic nature religion. In this form it honours the cycle of the years and the feasts of the seasons. It does not necessarily coincide with the witchcraft and magic of the degree of power described here, but this does not diminish its status.

DO IT YOURSELF?

It may come as no surprise that there are very few activities suggested here for the 'do-it-yourselfer'. Witchcraft is a particularly no-nonsense realm, and even with these modest suggestions, there must come the warning that, when engaging the powers of nature in this way, you must be responsible for the results, even those not anticipated.

An example of this comes from a situation involving the burning of candles. In a movie which was being made, the script required the main character to consult a Latin male witch, called a *brujo*, and engage him to do a spell for her. When that scene was being shot in front of the cameras, the actor who was playing the brujo began to behave oddly and aggressively to the crew members working on the film. When the director called 'cut', meaning the actors were to stop performing, the brujo carried on and eventually had to be restrained. It was an amazing and inexplicable situation. The production company consulted a real brujo to see if they could find out what had happened. When told how the scene had been shot and what candles had been used, he was not surprised at the result they got, as they had used the wrong colour candles and called forth dangerous powers!

Even with the 'simplest' magic, it is necessary to be very careful.

KINDS OF MAGIC YOU CAN DO

Wishes Making wishes is so common they may not seem magical. Yet when attention is focused, and particularly if the process is turned into a ritual, with something offered as the wish is made (remember tossing the coin in the fountain?) this is simple magic.

Candles The burning of candles to represent prayers for oneself or others, or for purification, is common to many religions. It is also a simple ritual you can perform. The candle to be burned must be blessed to the intention. Name the desired result with focused intent as the candle is lit. Normally certain colours are used for particular desires; rose for love, green for money, white for healing and purifying.

Pictures A picture of someone can be used to communicate with them. Love or healing can be sent or they can be asked for something, or to do something. Improperly used, this technique can influence others' personal will, so remember the magical warning – the subject need not accept the spell, and if it is rejected, it comes home to its maker!

Salt There are many substances which are considered 'magical insulators'. Salt is certainly the cheapest. Scattered across portals, doorways, windows and the like it will help repel not only negative energies, but also individuals who are not beneficial of character.

Protection – holy water, etc. Blessed materials carried the power and protection of the deity in whose name the blessing was asked. Any object which has been sanctified in this manner will radiate protection and blessing. Elements such as holy water and blessed incense can be used to clear the environment of unpleasant elements after, for instance, a visit by those who are a bit unsavoury.

RITUAL IN YOUR LIFE

Though it is not likely that many will become initiated makers of magic, there is value in learning to sense and appreciate the range of the powers of magic. When seeing any ritual, from a christening to a coronation, you will be able to appreciate the power behind each action in the process.

If interested in other countries and other cultures, it is possible to read about how ritual magic is used in each of them. If you are a student of Britain's folk traditions, explore what is understood of the ritual sites of the ancient past.

We are living in a time in history where the power of magic and the traditional reverence for those who have learned of its hidden knowledge has been eclipsed. Yet these individuals often have a great deal to offer from their understanding of nature's powers. Perhaps with the growing interest in the metaphysics some appreciation for this knowledge and skill will return. And if it does, you will have been among the first to know about it.

16

Objects of Power:
Gems, Crystals, Amulets and Talismans

EYE-CATCHING WONDERS

A dazzling jewel on a woman's finger, a crystal on a table glittering in the sunlight, a rabbit's foot dangling on a key chain: each has a magnetic quality and a primitive fascination, and each has the potential to be an object of power. Today a large gemstone may only symbolise having enough resources to acquire it, a crystal may be an indication of being 'tuned in' to the New Age, a rabbit's foot may be only a lucky talisman carried for fun, yet some echo in all of us still responds to the potential power in each.

The power of these, and indeed of all objects of this sort, derives from beliefs dating from long ago. In those times objects were used to gain power, at first in the most direct and primitive ways, such as taking the weapons, or even the head, of an enemy to absorb his strengths and skills. Later the objects became symbolic, though no less imbued with power. Over the years, much has been forgotten about why particular objects are so valued, but the part of each of us which is still related to that ancient past responds unconsciously to the symbolism of objects of power.

Jewels, both those of great monetary value, usually referred to as 'precious', and those of value more for their aesthetic appeal, draw on an ancient tradition of the use of gems for protection and healing.

Today, quartz crystals are thought of when stones for healing are mentioned. These clear stones all grow naturally with the same distinctive six-sided shape, no matter how large or small, or whether they are growing singly or in a cluster of many.

Amulets are personal charms, usually intended for protection or healing. Ranging from rabbits' feet to stones to ward off the evil eye, some look like jewellery: rings, bracelets or pendants. Talismans are objects which have become imbued with power, either by tradition or by a ritual, and can be made from any type of material. Where amulets are normally primarily protective in their purpose, talismans are intended to give to their possessor power to control an aspect of their own life, or, as is often the case, some other person's.

OLD-TIME CHARMS

In the earliest societies, the roles of village head, priest, doctor and historian were combined in the shaman or medicine man or woman. These people normally kept order amongst the members of the society and were the tribal historians and keepers of remedies for the diseases of that era. They were treated with great respect because of their knowledge. Their medicine bag held not only plants and roots, but also objects of power such as stones, gems, and talismans. These objects themselves were revered by village members as symbols of the power and knowledge of the healer. The purposes of the rituals ranged from blessing a hunt to ensure a good catch, to initiating young people into adulthood, empowering warriors, to healing the sick and treating the injured.

As social structures within societies became more sophisticated, the various roles once performed by the shaman were taken by more than one person: the healer was separate from the priest or the headman. Each of these roles had its own symbols of power or talismans. The medicine man had his bag of healing stones and herbs;

the priest and king had jewels as symbols of their positions
– the priest's worn on his vestments of office, the king's
on his regalia.

BIBLICAL GEMS

The Bible tells us the High Priest Aaron (Exodus 28:15–21)
was given instructions to make a breastplate of gold with
twelve stones, specified as ruby, topaz, beryl, turquoise,
sapphire, emerald, jacinth, agate, amethyst, chrysolite,
onyx, and jasper, each engraved with the name of one of
the twelve tribes of Israel. This was to be worn over his
heart, to enable him to make decisions on behalf of all the
Israelites. Though stones, gems and amulets have been
found in burial sites dating far back into antiquity, their
purpose had not been understood by archaeologists. This
is one of the first examples of a clear statement of their use
as amulets, as objects of power.

Priests have continued this tradition of wearing stones and
other objects associated with their role. An example still in
use today is the bishop's purple ring of office. Today many
assume that the display of stones in religious vestments is
a statement of the wealth of the Church. The original
reason for their presence has been forgotten; certain stones
were thought to enable the priest to fulfil his role more
powerfully. Naturally, if the priest was relied on to look
after the spiritual wellbeing of his flock, it was desirable
for him to have the best tools possible. So began the tradition of priests being provided with large stones and gems
to use in their work.

Similarly, in ancient times, the king was believed to be
the interpreter of divine will. Traditionally, it was also
believed that the king could heal with his touch. So naturally
the king would be provided with gems which would enable
him to better hear divine guidance. Because the divine
energies were believed to come in through the head, stones
were set so they could sit around the crown of the head,
the origin of the royal crown.

The original reason for the use of jewels by royalty was not to reflect the wealth or power of the wearer. Even today, it is impossible for anyone who has seen the Crown Jewels to forget their magnetic intensity. Not only are the brilliance of the stones and the rich lustre of the gold stunning and awe-inspiring, but there is also an unmistakable feeling of energy in these jewels that reaches beyond the position, power and value they represent.

SPARKLING SURPRISE

It is only since about 1500 that gemstones used in jewellery have been cut and faceted to reflect light and brilliance. Before then gemstones were polished to a smooth round surface, resulting in a jewel of deep velvety colour. This cut, called cabochon, is used rarely today.

It is curious to contemplate a large diamond as a polished lump of translucent white stone, or a ruby or emerald without sparkle, but this is in fact how all stones were used until the advent of cutting and faceting. The large central ruby on the Imperial State Crown, the Black Prince's Ruby, is uncut; it is a huge, though not glittering, centrepiece to that magnificent symbol of state.

VALUE BEYOND SPARKLE

The regalia of Great Britain are a fine example of the tradition of the use of stones, especially those set in precious metals, as objects of power. The State Crown has in it the previously mentioned ruby, as well as the Cullinan Diamond. These large stones, while impressive to look at, symbolise the energy of the sun (and astrologically is the correct planet for Leo, the sign of the zodiac associated with the sun and, symbolically, kings). These stones then draw to the monarch the appropriate energies for doing the job of being king or queen properly. The orb, a golden ball with a cross at the top of it, when held by the monarch, symbolises the acceptance of the divine guidance to the hand, as does the sceptre, with its large diamond drawing the divine light to it and to the hand that holds it.

EVERYDAY GEMS

The use of gems to attract proper energies was not limited to royalty and priests. Throughout the Middle Ages gems and stones were used as amulets, for their protective powers, and for healing. The knowledge of which stones to prescribe by looking at the patient's horoscope was considered a normal part of a doctor's education. This practice continues today in Asia, where it is common for an astrologer to suggest that an individual wear a particular stone. Sometimes the stone is prescribed for full-time wear to adjust the person's energies; at other times a particular stone will be suggested to balance the individual's energies during a time of particular stress. It is from the astrological diagnosis and use of specific stones to treat ailments peculiar to particular signs that 'birthstones' were derived. Today's birthstones are a far cry from those used medicinally, however.

For example, an executive with a very demanding job might be told to wear a ruby or a diamond on the left hand ring finger. This will draw the sun's energy into the system and strengthen it for a demanding schedule. The size of the stone is normally prescribed as well. It will usually be suggested that the stone be set so it touches the skin, and often the cabochon, or unfaceted, cut will be preferred. Sometimes the stone can be carried in the pocket, or worn as beads. A journalist travelling in an explosive part of the world was advised to carry hematite, a very heavy black stone which is believed to counteract an excess of Mars, the planet of war and explosions. This was to balance her energies and protect her from an excess of

Mars' energies while in a dangerous environment.

Metals alone are also used as amulets. Going far beyond the copper band seen around the wrist of many in the West, in the Orient rings, bracelets and even earrings of certain metals are suggested to balance the system. Combinations of gold, silver, copper, and lead are suggested and are so commonly used that it is easy to go into a jewellers in India to purchase a ring with the proper blend.

THE PROPERTIES OF STONES

The use of stones in healing is a foundation of ancient medicine. Holistic healers of the New Age are returning to the use of stones in this manner. This list is a combination of some of those pre-scientific attributes, plus some retained in tradition today. This list of attributes is from the *Crystal Awareness Guide*, published by the Legion of Light.

Amethyst Prevents drunkenness, protects against magic spells.
Aquamarine Protects travellers.
Diamond Strengthens and amplifies, clarifies thought, reflects will and power of God.
Emerald Strengthens immune system.
Jade Gives capacity to love, increases longevity and fertility.
Lapis lazuli Stimulates thyroid, relieves anxiety.
Malachite Heals physical injuries, gives warrior-like qualities.
Moonstone Increases intuition (and emotional vulnerability).
Opal Improves eyesight.
Onyx Grounding, strengthens bone marrow.
Pyrite ('fool's gold') Money attractor.
Ruby Gives courage and strength.
Sapphire Protection from snakebite.
Turquoise Aids tissue regeneration, vitalises blood.

BIRTHSTONES – TRADITIONAL

The traditional assignment of stones to the signs of the zodiac has evolved over thousands of years of use of stones as amulets. Each sign has a particular vibration. The stone associated with that sign has a similar vibration. This means, oddly enough, that a sign's birthstone will not always be the best choice for that sign to wear! For example, an already aggressive Aries may not want to increase energy by wearing a ruby, but would benefit from wearing a stone which brings out the more sensitive side, such as a moonstone.

Aries	Ruby, tourmaline, garnet.
Taurus	Sapphire, lapis lazuli.
Gemini	Topaz, citrine, amber.
Cancer	Pearl, moonstone.
Leo	Diamond, rock crystal.
Virgo	Topaz, tiger's eye, yellow sapphire.
Libra	Opal, smoky quartz.
Scorpio	Bloodstone, red garnet.
Sagittarius	Sapphire, amethyst.
Capricorn	Hematite, onyx, jet.
Aquarius	Aquamarine, turquoise.
Pisces	Amethyst.

BIRTHSTONES – CONTEMPORARY
(With thanks to *Gemstones of the World* by Walter Schumann, Sterling Publishing)

This list, developed by the gem industry, is a recent re-hashing of the traditional gems. While it is true that it may be more exciting for a Capricorn to receive a garnet ring as a birthday gift than one of black hematite, the stones no longer reflect the healing associations that gemstones once had with the signs of the zodiac. Note that not only are there substitutions, but some have had their positions changed entirely!

Aries	Diamond.
Taurus	Emerald.
Gemini	Pearl.
Cancer	Ruby.
Leo	Peridot.
Virgo	Sapphire.
Libra	Opal.
Scorpio	Topaz.
Sagittarius	Turquoise.
Capricorn	Garnet.
Aquarius	Amethyst.
Pisces	Aquamarine.

CRYSTAL CLEAR

The latest sensation of the New Age is crystals. As the term is now used in metaphysical circles, it refers to the clear minerals which grow in sizes ranging from the width of a tiny pin to the size of a man's thigh. They grow in clusters in caves in many parts of the world. However, by the time they find their way to the stores where they are sold, they have usually been separated into individual crystal 'points'. A point is one of the six-sided units of crystal.

Technically, crystals are considered to be gemstones like rubies, diamonds and emeralds. In fact some gemstones are actually coloured crystals: the best known among these are amethyst and rose quartz. It is the clear variety of crystal which is getting the most attention today. Though all stones and gems have characteristic energy properties of their own and absorb the energy of an individual who works with them or wears them, crystals are especially remarkable for these qualities.

Two elements, silicon and oxygen, combine into silicon dioxide to become quartz crystals. Small amounts of other elements in the composition give the coloured varieties of crystals, such as amethyst, their purple hue. Silica, one of the two elements in quartz, is also present in all glass, including the manufactured glass called 'crystal'. That glass, though it sparkles, is not useful as an energy-retaining gemstone because lead is included in its formula, which makes it stronger and clearer than ordinary glass, but reduces its energy-holding capacity to nil. So though a handblown crystal paperweight may sit prettily on your desk, it will not have the energy potential that a naturally grown and mined quartz crystal has.

The capacity of quartz crystals to store and amplify energy has resulted in their wide use in industry. They respond by oscillating, or vibrating, at a predictable rate depending on the electricity used. By exact measurement of the size of the quartz crystal and the amount of current applied, crystals can be used to transform electricity into radio and television waves, and are used in the precise timing mechanisms in quartz watches.

Cousins of quartz crystals, silicon chips, are used in computers. In much the same way as crystals are used in watches, the crystal structure of silicon combined with very delicately metred electricity allows computers to store information and process data. This can be compared to the way quartz crystals used for metaphysical purposes can store information and energy, gather and amplify it, and even be programmed to release it. The electrical source in this case, however, is the energy field of the person using the crystal.

ENERGY ABSORBERS

It is the crystal's ability to 'remember' energy which makes it so useful and equally easy to misuse. Today crystals are most commonly seen resting on tables, for decorative purposes or for protection as an energy absorber. They also frequently appear as amulets in the form of earrings and pendants.

Left out in the open in a room, crystals indiscriminately absorb all the energies around them — the atmosphere of the room itself, the emotional state of anyone in the room.

In the case of a crystal which is being worn, it not only absorbs the feelings of the person wearing it, but those of anyone with whom they come into close contact. As crystals will radiate the energies they have absorbed, they need to be cleansed of negative energies from time to time.

CRYSTAL HOUSEKEEPING

There are several methods for cleaning crystals, some quick, others more time-consuming. First, take a good look at the crystal. When crystals have absorbed energies, particularly negative ones, they acquire a greasy and muddy appearance. It almost seems as if they had been handled by someone with dirty hands. If a crystal has that appearance, it needs to be cleaned.

Crystals can be cleaned in water, sunlight, salt or earth. The methods are listed in ascending order of power.

Water Either place the crystal in fresh water in a bowl or hold it under running cold tap water, or ideally in a running stream. If placing the crystal in the bowl, leave it overnight, but in running water for just a minute. Either method will give it a fresh glow.

Sunlight Simply place the crystal in a direct beam of sunlight for a day or two. This is only for clear crystals, because coloured crystals such as amethysts and rose quartz will fade in sunlight!

Salt Bury the crystal completely in coarse unrefined salt. Depending on how muddy the stone looked, it may be necessary to leave it for as long as a week.

Earth This is the most intense way of cleaning any stone. Bury the crystal in the earth outside, not in a potted plant. Three days to two weeks will do the trick. Do mark where it has been put in some way, so as not to lose track of it.

(Note – all these methods will also cleanse jewellery, perhaps old pieces inherited from someone whose energy you do not also wish to inherit or pieces purchased with an unknown background. Do not put pieces of jewellery set in metal in salt, because the salt may react chemically with materials in the metal and tarnish it badly.)

At the end of any of these processes the crystal should sparkle and have clear shiny surfaces. It should have none of that greasy feel left, but should somehow seem radiant.

PUT YOUR CRYSTAL TO WORK

There are two basic ways in which crystals are used: passively and actively. Most crystals have passive roles, sitting in rooms and in jewellery, as sort of cosmic air conditioners. They absorb energies and vibrations just by being what they are.

There are two active ways to use crystals. One is to 'program' them by directing specific thoughts or energy at them. They will then radiate that energy back into the environment. This is like recording sound on a blank tape and then playing it back. The other active way crystals are used is in the hand of a healer or other practitioner who uses them to amplify the energy they are projecting. In this way the energy moves through the crystal to the subject.

PROGRAMMING A CRYSTAL

Crystals are so easy to program that you may have done it without knowing it. Because they will absorb all energy around them, thoughts, which are only a form of electrical energy, are readily taken in by crystals. Always clean a crystal before programming or charging it.

The first step is to focus clearly on the intention of the program. It may be easier to write it down. Then take the crystal in the hand you use to write with, which is called your dominant hand. If the crystal is large, hold that hand over it. Concentrate on the intended program, or read what is written down, calmly and clearly stating what you wish the crystal to do or what energy you wish it to radiate. Talk to it as if it were a friend if that is easier.

An interesting way to determine if the crystal has been correctly programmed is to ask a friend who has no knowledge of the instructions to hold the crystal and tell you what comes immediately to their mind. If they are even slightly intuitive, they should come up with something similar to the focus of the intention in your program.

USES FOR CRYSTALS

Cleansing

Environment Place the crystal in a room and allow it passively to collect the energies.

Program the crystal to radiate the desired feeling and place it in a room. For example, if you want your dinner guests to feel comfortable and at ease, program the crystal that way.

Program the crystal to collect unpleasant and negative energies – very useful for any room where people must wait and might be a bit nervous. The crystal will help calm them.

Personal Place the crystal in the evening bath water and allow it to wash away the day's acquired negative energies. Charge it with that power before putting it in the water if you wish.

Growth and Mental Expansion

Program the crystal to help with having clear dreams and to remembering them easily. Leave it by the bed as you sleep.

If you plan to have a meeting, an important chat, or a session with a therapist, program your crystal for mental clarity and set it out near where you will be.

If having difficult house guests, program the crystal for

them to feel happy during their stay and leave it lovingly in their room.

Put a calmingly programmed crystal in the room with a sick child so he can rest more easily and be less fussy.

Health

Healing If you have a headache or a pain, place the crystal on or near that spot, programmed to absorb the energy.

Place a crystal programmed for healing on a photograph of someone whom you wish to heal.

For a wound or injury direct a crystal to bring fresh, healing energy to that spot.

If a friend is ill, use the crystal by scanning with it in one hand over the person's body, sending loving, positive healing thoughts.

Cleansing After surgery or treatment by drugs, place a crystal programmed to cleanse the system near the body to aid in eliminating toxins from the system.

Spiritual

Meditation Crystals enhance and focus the meditative state. Position a crystal nearby while meditating.

Consciousness expansion If feeling spiritually blocked, program the crystal to help see where those blocks are and to melt them. Then sit quietly with the crystal nearby and see what comes to mind.

WHERE TO BUY YOUR CRYSTAL

Many stores now sell crystals in their gift departments. Often they make pretty and not too pricey gifts. For personal use, there are stores specialising in crystals. Old-fashioned mineral collector's stores will have a wide selection of quartz crystals on hand, but will view them as a not particularly special part of the range of goods. Personnel at such stores are unlikely to be informed enough to answer any metaphysical questions. There might be a New Age store, sometimes a book store which will also stock crystals, and with luck, perhaps a crystal speciality store. With the increasing interest in crystals, there are now even mail order crystal supply companies.

HOW TO SELECT YOUR CRYSTAL

The first visit to a crystal store is overwhelming. Even if you don't believe a thing about the power of crystals, the range of shape, colour and size is astonishing. The characteristics of crystals are:

Colour Clear quartz is the most usual, but many stores have other varieties of coloured quartz, and also other stones which come in crystalline form.

Clarity The difference between a small, but very clear stone, and a larger but more cloudy one is remarkable. Most crystals are cloudy near their base. Sometimes they have fractures in the middle as well.

Size and Quantity Crystals grow to a wide range of sizes. They are usually left the size they were found, rather than being cut as gemstones normally are. They grow in clusters, most of which are broken up when the crystals are mined. Occasionally a cluster of a few to as many as twenty crystals will stay together. The larger ones are magnificent and usually expensive as well.

Feeling The intangible quality is the major guide in selecting a crystal. Unlike a precious jewel such as a diamond, which is graded and priced by rigid standards, the selection of a crystal is subjective, as it needs to 'fit' your vibrations; only you can feel which one is suitable. One may be more attractive visually, but another will feel more comfortable. Take the comfortable one home.

CHARMS AND TALISMANS

Every culture has objects traditionally symbolising luck and good fortune, and those that bode ill. These objects change from culture to culture, which can be very confusing for someone who moves to a new country.

Rabbits' feet, four-leaf clovers, horseshoes, a shiny new penny all bring a reassuring smile to the face in our culture. These are charms, so called because they once were put under a spell or 'charm'. In a manner not unlike the way in which a crystal is programmed, the maker of the spell or charm imbues the object with the desired energy. The purpose of this is to attract a desired result to a subject, with or without their knowledge.

SINISTER SHADOWS

The darker side of charms and talismans is that of black witchcraft, which puts a spell on another person without his knowledge or permission. Usually a picture or a possession of the individual is necessary. This is why people of many native cultures, that still have an awareness of traditions of this sort will not allow tourists to take their photographs.

The voodoo doll of fiction comes under this category. Usually dressed in clothes cut from cloth of a possession of the subject, the doll is subjected to rituals intended to symbolise the sort of events the spellmaker desires to happen to the victim.

Outside an anthropological museum, you are unlikely to run into many voodoo dolls in contemporary Europe. Take a look around, though. Creatures ranging from gargoyles on churches to gnomes watching over gardens have their origin as protective talismans.

GOOD LUCK

Before he was demoted, Saint Christopher had a busy time as the protector of travellers. He appeared on key chains, in cars, anywhere travellers went. He was a talisman thought to assure safety by bringing his saintly energy to the user. Religious figures of this sort act as 'stand-ins' for the blessings which those saints are reputed to give and are talismans.

Figures of reverence, such as statues which have stood in public places over a long period of time, become full of the energy of the faithful. The strong sense of power often evident when visiting a shrine is because the objects of veneration have absorbed so much energy that they are now reflecting it back to the faithful.

CREATING LUCK

Talismans and amulets usually take one of two forms. The first is to have the image of the desired result. For example, an amulet for fertility will resemble a very pregnant woman; in some cultures coins are given to babies or to newly married couples to symbolise wealth.

The second is to symbolise an object which will protect the user from danger. In Mediterranean countries cars and trucks are hung with protective talismans, often in the form of an eye. A general all-purpose spell protector, the eye is found throughout the world doing duty as a talismanic watchdog.

Athletes, particularly jockeys, are famous for having their own personal talismanic objects. A sock worn when an important race was won, a coin in a pocket, these objects become imbued with the power of the belief of the person who owns them that they do radiate the 'luck' they expect back to them, just like crystals.

Many already have their own talismans – a paperweight which must be on the desk before a letter can be written, a picture of a loved one which travels everywhere. Those who don't have one can make one. Select an object which feels truly comfortable, for example a driver might choose a special charm to put on a key chain. Holding it, bless it and ask for protection. Presto, a homemade talisman! As it is used, it will become more powerful.

A CHARMED FUTURE?

This completes your conducted tour of the realm of objects of power. Now it is possible to make a choice of which ones to use and become more familiar with; perhaps crystals to increase and direct energy, or jewels, which will have a new meaning as their power as well as their beauty is appreciated. The strange world of talismans and charms is no longer a mystery. Perhaps you can look forward to a charmed future.

17

Meditation

Does learning to meditate seem an appealing idea? It does to many. The enquirer will, early on, encounter rumours, as to both the benefits of meditation and its demands. Associated with it are images of bearded gurus, sounds of foreign syllables, peculiar postures required of disciples; tales are diverse, and often exploration only results in more mysteries and hearsay. Meditation itself could not be more straightforward. It is a single discipline, yet because there are many philosophies behind it and methods of approach, confusion surrounds it. There are three primary sources of this confusion.

One is the word itself, meditation. It has a more general use, meaning to think or reflect. Until it is clear that the practice of meditation is a specific activity, quite different from 'thinking', much of what is said about what it has to offer will not make sense.

Many who are interested in knowing more are confused about where to go to learn about it; for them meditation may only be associated with Eastern spiritual studies. Is it then necessary to go to an Eastern-orientated centre to learn it, and must it have religious overtones? Can those who have an interest but no religious belief do it?

The third, based on the second confusion, is the concern about being drawn into strange or foreign practices, into more religion than may be one's inclination, or of having to say peculiar syllables or sit in uncomfortable positions in order to meditate.

In spite of these concerns, many study and start to meditate each year. Learn what those who begin the practice do, why and what they get from it.

DO YOU MEDITATE ALREADY?

Meditation does live up to the claims to be beneficial; it results in being calmer and more comfortable within oneself. While it is true that meditation, as the term is used in the spiritual sense, does usually involve training, many will be surprised to find they have already been in the meditative state many times in their lives without realising it.

You have probably been in the state yourself. It does not only occur in a seated position with the eyes closed. Anyone who has ever been completely lost in doing a task, or perhaps in listening or to playing music, or so absorbed in working in a garden that the sense of time and place were lost; or concentrating so much that the approach of someone startled them, was most likely a meditative state.

STATES OF MIND

Very rarely does any of us ever stop and think about what we think. We just don't notice the chatter which rattles along ceaselessly in our brains, sometimes helping us make our way through the day, absorbed in analysing the past, looking at the future, reacting to situations as they arise. The mind ticks away, occasionally focused in organising life, but usually easily swayed by whatever crosses our vision.

There are specific states of mind – these are not just moods. It is obvious that the mind is not in the same state when awake as when asleep, but the waking mind itself also has different states, distinct enough to be measured scientifically.

The brain emits electrical waves in rhythmic patterns

which differ between the various states. These waves can be measured. When sleeping, gamma waves are emitted; those with very little brain activity, who are unconscious or in a coma, emit delta waves. There are also two waking states: everyday thought is indicated by beta waves, and alpha waves or rhythms indicate relaxed but alert attention. These are associated with being at ease or engaged in some sort of creative activity; this is also the brain-wave pattern displayed in meditation. It has physical characteristics as well. The body is relaxed, breathing slows and blood pressure drops. Signs of stress diminish, and the production of the hormone adrenaline, which occurs as the result of anxiety, drops.

When alpha rhythms are emitted in activities in everyday life, such as when relaxing, playing music, or creative endeavours, they are but a fortunate 'side effect'. The aim of meditation is to create that state. 'Learning to meditate' teaches you how to be mentally alert and focused yet relaxed.

I'LL MEDITATE ON THAT!

Those who do it say the state of mind which is known as meditation feels wonderful. Some say meditation refreshes as much as a good nap. Individuals who have work or hobbies which bring about a meditative state obtain its benefits just by doing what they enjoy. Even though they may be physically tiring ones, such as gardening, they will still give a feeling of being refreshed and restored because of the relaxation which results from being in that state of mind. It is not essential that meditation be done when physically still. In fact in many Buddhist monasteries, where meditation features as a large part of the day, meditation is done while walking.

There are many approaches and methods of study, and a variety of worthwhile techniques. To better understand it, let's look at the progression of mental states before and after the meditative one.

Unconsciousness or coma Unresponsive to outside stimulus or activity; occurs when 'knocked out' or under anaesthetic. This state normally results from outside intervention such as a blow to the head or the administration of certain drugs.

Sleep Not conscious and unaware of normal background activities, yet will respond to a strong outside stimulus.

Consciousness Aware, unfocused mental state in which the mind is responsive to outside influences which easily cause the focus of attention to be shifted.

Attention The state in which the mind is focused on the thought or task at hand, but can still be distracted.

Concentration The mind is focused by choice on the thought or task and is not easily distracted.

Meditation The mind focuses intently and effortlessly on the thought or task, and is distracted only by intense stimulation.

Contemplation The mind is lost in absorption in the objective, sense of self and personal individuality being lost for the moment.

Samadhi The merging of the individual mind with the object of focus, the state identified with religious ecstasy.

(This list is adapted from Ernest Wood's *Concentration*, Quest Books.)

JUST TRY CONCENTRATION

Those who begin to observe the mind first notice what an unruly thing it can be. Before approaching the techniques which are used to attain a meditative state, simply take a look at how difficult it is to concentrate. The great Indian sage, Ramakrishna, described the mind as being like 'a chattering monkey swinging from branch to branch'. Getting the mind to stay in one place is more of a project than might at first be imagined.

In an exercise from his excellent book on meditation,

called, aptly enough *Concentration*, Ernest Wood suggests an experiment to see how well you can keep your mind in one spot by focusing on, for example, a cat. Think of a series of things associated with 'cat', and always return to the subject of focus, 'cat'. You might think of cat, then whisker; cat, then fur; cat, then claw; cat, then milk. And when thinking of milk the mind might also say, 'Oh my, I need milk, must stop when I'm next at the shop. Oh, and light bulbs too . . .' and the mind is off and running. See how it works for yourself! Some good topics for practising focusing are a drinking mug, a flower, or a book.

The first time most people do this exercise, they are astonished to see how quickly the mind skitters away from them. The fact is very few people have developed the capacity to concentrate without a forceful focal point, such as a compellingly interesting programme on television or an intense conversation with a friend. Yet all of us have had moments when we were concentrating with such focus that we didn't even notice outside events or the passage of time.

Again, the difference is the intention. One of the first steps to meditation is learning concentration. If wanting to learn to meditate on your own, a good starting point is watching the mind's antics as it chatters away and practise keeping it in line and focused.

ROSARIES AND NAVELS

Having seen how quickly the mind wanders from the topic at hand, it is easy to imagine why many prefer to meditate using an object as a point of focus. The hobbyist who is intent on his ship model is an example. As long as he is putting together the pieces, he is lost in his work and need not 'discipline' his mind to concentrate.

Almost every religion has some form of 'rosary', or beads which are used to count one's prayers. The repetition of the prayers and the counting of the beads engage the mind and the body, making it easier to keep the concentration focused. While it is possible for the mind to wander while engaged in the counting of the beads, sooner or later the physical counting will stop, alerting the individual to his inattentiveness.

There used to be jokes about yogis 'contemplating their navels'. It may seem an odd part of the anatomy on which to dwell in pursuit of spiritual progress, but recent experiments in meditation and the study of the brain waves using a biofeedback machine have proved that focusing on a body part is one of the best ways to still the mind enough to bring on the meditative state.

BLOOD PRESSURE AND BRAIN WAVES

Desperate to find ways to reduce the dangerous levels of blood pressure in their patients because many of the drugs employed to lower blood pressure have undesirable side-effects, doctors have turned to meditation as a treatment for this condition. Using biofeedback machines, which monitor minute changes in the body's state, patients are provided with immediate information about changes in the blood pressure, respiration rate, and heartbeat as the result of altered mental states. Because the machine gives a signal when the desired state is attained, or 'feedback to the body', the patient learns quickly what mental state produces the desired relaxed state as opposed to the habitual stressed condition.

The surprising fact is that if the biofeedback machine is attached to, for instance, the little finger, so the pulse and other physical responses are measured from that point in the body. Concentration on lowering the blood pressure at that point results in changes in the entire body's pressure. By changing the state of the little finger alone, enough so it registers on the machine, you can change the whole body's response. That is not far from the proverbial yogi contemplating his navel, and the yogi would certainly have the same relaxation response. No matter what part of the body is focused on, even the navel, the entire body responds and relaxes.

WORDS AND SOUND

Meditation has been associated with chanting and the use of sound, with a particular emphasis on those which seem to the British ear a bit peculiar. Two types of sounds are used in meditation, repetitive sound and focusing sound. The reader of a rosary, saying prayers, whether in the Orient or the West, or the monk sitting in the monastery chanting, use the sound to still the mind and to keep the attention while in the meditative state. In group meditation, the sounds will be repeated with a certain hypnotic cadence to produce a group meditative state. The repetition may go on for hours. While the sounds made in an Eastern setting may seem very strange, they are usually a prayer not unlike the Catholic 'Hail Mary'.

When sound is employed as a technique to focus the mind, an individual or a group will start out using repetition as well. As the state of meditation is achieved, the sounding will stop and the remainder of the process will continue in silence.

The word or words used to attain the meditative state are called mantras in the East. In some training programmes for meditation, especially those originating from India, the giving of the mantra is a very important ceremony, and the mantra is meant to be kept privately to oneself. In mystical Judaism there is a study of the powers of words and sound and it is believed that certain words have great power if uttered out loud. This gives the impression that it is the specific word that has the power. The fact is that any word can be used as a mantra. It is true that some words, in use for a very long time, symbolise indelibly to us a spiritual idea. Naturally, the words we recognise come from our own culture. In mantras of Indian origin, the words used are generally Sanskrit, a now unused ancient language of India. It is the mother tongue of India's

244

contemporary language, Hindi, just as Latin is to the Romance languages in the West. The most often used word is OM, a syllable which is meant to be the vibration of the universe. By chanting this, you would be able to tune in to that vibration.

OBJECTS OF CONTEMPLATION

Most places of worship have figures in the form of paintings and sculptures. While these figures are decorative, they are often intended to be objects of contemplation. These objects can stand as strongly evocative symbols of the ideal of the religion, as well as being points on which the mind can focus while meditating. Sometimes this meditation focuses on developing the qualities attributed to the ideal whose form is portrayed: the forgiveness of the Virgin Mary, the power of the Indian god, Shiva, the compassion of the Buddha. The form of the objects may be completely symbolic, such as the beautifully embellished Arabic writing seen in Islamic mosques, in which the names of the Prophet will be written to inspire the meditator to contemplate his characteristics.

Often meditators will have an altar at home with similar objects to focus on for private practice. They may choose an object of personal meaning on which to meditate. It could be an image of a deity, or an apparently ordinary-looking item such as a seashell or a rock which symbolises a desired quality or reminds the meditator of an important moment. For them that object will be as powerful a focus of attention as any more traditional one would be.

MIND AS MANTRA

Some forms of meditation use the mind itself as the object of focus. Zen, a branch of Buddhism, calls meditation 'sitting'. In it the 'sitter' quietly observes the mind as it chatters away, actually using it as a mantra would be used. The intention is that as the mind is observed its antics become boring and eventually the awareness comes as you watch your mind, that you are not the mind, but the watcher! Zen meditation is usually accompanied by the study of a series of koans, riddles given by the Zen Master to his student to contemplate while watching his mind. One of the best-known koans is 'What is the sound of one hand clapping?'

All these techniques are designed to acquaint the meditator with the mind and its tricks and to give techniques to gain control over the mind so as to focus properly in order to be able to meditate.

MEDITATION GROUPS

There is great advantage to starting out meditating in a group. The obvious ones are making a commitment of time and place, and being in an environment where there will not be the distraction of the phone ringing, or the dog nuzzling to go for a walk just when you've finally settled down.

In a group you will sit for a period of time, usually from twenty minutes to an hour, with others who are there to meditate as well. Quiet will be maintained and there will be someone to start the session and bell or gong at the end. Worries about time or environment are relieved, aiding in the relaxation necessary for meditation.

The second benefit comes from what might be called the 'group energy'. It seems it is much easier to concentrate when those around you have the same aim. Many beginners who have not sufficiently strengthened the 'muscle' of concentration find it impossible to focus long enough when trying to meditate on their own, but feel the benefit of the support of the group.

As the meditative state is an unfamiliar one to most, starting out in a group also allows the exchange of experiences with others who are beginning as well as with the instructor. This makes it easy to find out whether any problems are normal, how to solve them, how to pace your practice and what to expect as a result of your efforts.

PASS THE PRETZELS

One worry that many people have is that meditation will require sitting on the floor in a peculiar cross-legged position which will be miserably uncomfortable! Experienced meditators find certain positions do make meditation easier, but it isn't necessary to bend up like a pretzel to meditate. There are some helpful points for beginners, however.

First of all, do not try to meditate lying down. It may be relaxing, but it is an invitation to fall asleep. If there is one rule which must be followed, this is it. Meditation does need to be done in an upright position. There are two requirements for the meditative posture; one that the body is in a balanced position, and second that the back be straight. Because meditation as a regular practice is more common in Oriental religions, where the everyday habit is to sit on the floor with crossed legs, meditation has traditionally been taught in this position.

It terrifies the average Westerner just to look at the extreme seated meditation posture, which is called the lotus position. It is the 'pretzel' posture most people imagine when they think of a person meditating, on the floor with legs not only crossed, but with each foot resting firmly on the opposite thigh. The advantage of this is that the locked position of the feet near the groin allows the individual to sit perfectly balanced with a straight back. In this position, once a state of deep meditation is attained, it isn't necessary to adjust the posture. Some Westerners with stiff hip joints find they can manage to sit on the floor with crossed legs if they have a 'meditation cushion' under their bottoms. This is a very firm small round cushion which, placed under the buttocks only, not the legs, lifts the hips off the floor and removes uncomfortable stress on rigid hip joints.

While it may be traditional, it is not at all necessary to sit in a cross-legged position to meditate, or even on the floor. Remember, some meditation is done while walking (and there is even a monastery in Japan in which the meditator rakes rocks!) For seated meditation, the normal Western chair is not the best choice because it is too easy to slump and the back must be kept straight. A cushion placed behind the small of the back may give enough support to keep the spine sufficiently straight.

It may take some experimentation, but eventually you will find a comfortable position, balanced, with the spine straight and supported enough to sit for a time comfortably.

TEACHERS, GURUS AND GROUPS

There are many places to go and ways to learn meditation. For the rugged individualist, libraries and booksellers will have books on learning to meditate. Some, published by individual groups and teachers, will show just the one approach and method they advocate. A book of this type would be good if having to make a choice among different techniques sounds too confusing. Other books, by individual students who have studied with a variety of teachers but are not aligned with any one particular group, will offer a range of ideas and views based on the author's sampling and experience. They will have a choice of methods and techniques.

For those who prefer to learn with a group, meditation classes are sometimes available at local colleges, universities and adult education schools. They are also offered by the groups and religions which include meditation as part of their philosophy. Both types of classes can be found listed in magazines and newspapers which describe what's going on in town. And, as usual, a bookshop which specialises in metaphysical topics will be a great source for finding classes and groups.

Because meditation is an important part of the study of some types of the Buddhist religion, a local Buddhist society will usually offer both classes for training and have ongoing meditation groups.

There are some groups in which the meditation technique

taught is unique to the group or the teacher or guru (teacher in the Indian language of Sanskrit). These are strongly stamped with the personality of the leader. One of these may be appealing and the atmosphere and the methods taught will be comfortable. Remember, though, the people who are already there as part of the group, who are commonly called devotees, will tend to feel rather strongly that their teacher and the teacher's way of doing things is the best, bar none. If you don't feel comfortable with their approach, don't let their enthusiasm shake your conviction if you feel the need to explore further. There are some meditation groups which are quite dedicated to proselytising, the members believing that they achieve merit for themselves by bringing others into the group. These people can be downright pushy in their tactics, and it is important you remember your right to say no if you run into one of these groups and are not comfortable with their approach and techniques.

RESULTS

The reduction of stress alone is a wonderful benefit from meditation. In individuals where stress has created physical problems, such as high blood pressure, it is marvellous to have a natural method to combat the condition.

Meditation does have other results; and some groups promise further benefits. It seems that all types of meditation calm the reactions of the nervous system. Not only are the physical results of stress reduced, but mental stress is reduced as well. Meditators report that situations that would have had them running screaming down the road before they started can now be dealt with calmly. These results take some time to develop, certainly three to six months of regular meditation.

Some groups promise and focus on certain types of benefits. One group promises anything you want by doing their form of meditation – not just lowered blood pressure, but that new sports car! Several promise enhanced psychic abilities, and one suggests their type of meditation will eventually enable you to levitate – yes, to float in the air. If these results interest you, then these are the groups for you. But listen to this tale.

THE MAN WHO KNEW TOO MUCH –
FROM MEDITATING

A man who is a government official in India, a country where meditation is not an uncommon practice, learned a new form of meditation from a guru, or teacher. He was to sit quietly with his middle finger on his forehead and his first and third fingers gently pressing on his closed eyes. Do this twice a day, he was told, and he would have amazing results. A practical man, he liked the idea of dramatic results, so he took the time from his busy schedule to pursue his meditation practice, as he was told, twice a day. Soon he did begin to notice the results that he had been promised. He began to become very psychic. He would know who was on the phone when it rang, who would be coming to see him, what people were about to say. He found he was always right. And he gave up that form of meditation. He said he found it boring to know everything that was going to happen before it did!

THE REAL REASON TO MEDITATE

The differing meditation teachers and groups lure the beginner with a variety of personalities, techniques and promises. Depending on the desires of the student, the attraction of the promised results is more likely to keep them persistent in their practice than sheer self-discipline. Once the novelty is over, it does take a bit of character to sit down and meditate. And it does take some months for the benefits to become apparent.

There is a second set of benefits which appear after a longer period of meditation – sometimes after years of it. And this is what brings together all the various types of meditation with their various goals. All types of meditation, even the ones which start out with the acquisition of a Mercedes Benz as the focus, ultimately result in a deepening of the spiritual nature. This connection with that nature allows one to live life in a more centred, peaceful way and to be able to look on life's ups and downs with a calm eye.

If you wish to try out meditating, then don't be afraid you won't do it properly, or you will not select the right kind. It appears that all paths end in the same spot, and that spot is a very peaceful place indeed.

Bibliography

Anderson, Mary, *Palmistry, Your Destiny in Your Hands*, Thorsons, 1980

Bradbury, Will (Ed.), *Into the Unknown*, Reader's Digest, 1988

Gettings, Fred, *Secret Symbolism in Occult Art*, Harmony Books, 1987

Goodman, Linda, *Sun Signs*, Harrap, 1970

Grey, Eden, *Mastering the Tarot*, Signet, 1971

Healki, Thomas, *Creative Ritual*, Samuel Weiser, 1986

Ho, Palmer and O'Brien, *Lines of Destiny*, Shambala, 1986

Hole, Christina, *Witchcraft in Britain*, Paladin, 1977

How to Tell Your Fortune, Martin Cavendish Books Ltd, 1985

Legion of Light, *Crystal Awareness Guide*, Legion of Light Products, 1987

Locke, Stephen, MD, and Colligan, Douglas, *The Healer Within*, Mentor, 1986

Regan, Georgina, and Shapiro, Debbie, *The Healer's Handbook*, Element Books Ltd, 1988

Schumann, Walter, *Gemstones of the World*, Sterling Publishing, 1984

Villoldo, Alberto, and Krippner, Stanley, *Healing States*, Fireside Books, 1986

Walker, Charles, *The Occult Atlas of Great Britain*, Hamlyn, 1987

Wood, Ernest, *Concentration*, Quest Books, 1979

MIND TO MIND
by Betty Shine

Her extraordinary gifts — a clairvoyant ability to diagnose medically, her healing powers and her discovery of 'mind energy' — have made her one of Britain's foremost healers.

MIND TO MIND tells her story. Like Betty herself, it is cheerful, down-to-earth and full of humour. It reveals how she became aware of her gifts and how she has used her experiences of mind energy to help others. Illustrated with a wide variety of examples and case histories, this is uniquely helpful and practical book by a woman whose powers have been a comfort and an inspiration to countless numbers of people.

'It is a positive, optimistic book, which I am sure will be a great encouragement to anyone who believes that the mind is capable of much more than we can presently dream of'
Michael Aspel

'This is a rare book, written by a rare person. I know that you will enjoy reading it'
Michael Bentine

'Full of fascinating case histories'
Guardian

'Fascinating and very readable . . . compelling and informative . . . written with humility and intelligence'
Psychic News

0 552 13378 7

THE FURTHER PROPHECIES OF NOSTRADAMUS
by Erika Cheetham

Many of the prophecies contained in The Centuries of 16th Century astrologer and seer Michel de Nostredame have already come true . . .

In this fascinating and deeply-researched sequel to the international bestseller, THE PROPHECIES OF NOSTRADAMUS, Erika Cheetham focuses attention on Nostradamus' view of our present world and what is to come:

WAR IN THE MIDDLE EAST
THE GROWTH IN MILITARY MIGHT OF THE THREE GREAT POWERS
THE RISE OF THE THIRD ANTI-CHRIST FROM THE EAST
THE END OF THE PAPACY
A VAST EARTHQUAKE IN THE U.S.A.
THE END OF THE BRITISH MONARCHY

0 552 12299 8

KNOW YOUR OWN PSI-Q
by Hans Eysenck & Carl Sargent

Do you have psychic powers?
Do you sense the unseen?
Do you imagine events before they happen?

For the first time KNOW YOUR OWN PSI-Q gives you the key to the mysterious world of psychic energy.

Start with the self-testing questionnaire to find out whether your personality indicates receptivity to Psi forces. Then proceed to the simple games which require nothing more than a dice and a pack of cards . . . soon you will have a complete profile of the hidden psychic powers of your mind.

Research into parapsychology has rapidly progressed in recent years and scientists have now formulated many new ways of measuring psychic efforts. The tests and exercises included in this book are based on laboratory experiments carried out by the leading experts in the field.

0 552 12772 8

A SELECTION OF NON-FICTION TITLES AVAILABLE FROM CORGI BOOKS

☐	99160 0	**FIRE FROM WITHIN**	*Carlos Casteneda*	£3.95
☐	99332 8	**THE POWER OF SILENCE**	*Carlos Casteneda*	£3.99
☐	12299 8	**THE FURTHER PROPHECIES OF NOSTRADAMUS**	*Erika Cheetham*	£2.95
☐	09828 0	**THE PROPHECIES OF NOSTRADAMUS**	*Erika Cheetham*	£3.99
☐	12772 8	**KNOW YOUR OWN PSI-Q**	*Hans Eysenck & Carl Sargent*	£2.50
☐	07145 5	**THE THIRD EYE**	*T. Lobsang Rampa*	£2.99
☐	11487 1	**LIFE AFTER DEATH**	*Neville Randall*	£2.75
☐	13378 7	**MIND TO MIND**	*Betty Shine*	£3.50
☐	13429 5	**THE AFTER DEATH EXPERIENCE**	*Ian Wilson*	£3.99